cool architecture

cool architecture

designing for cold climates

images
Publishing

Published in Australia in 2003 by
The Images Publishing Group Pty Ltd
ACN 059 734 431
6 Bastow Place, Mulgrave, Victoria 3170, Australia
Telephone (61 3) 9561 5544 Facsimile (61 3) 9561 4860
Email: books@images.com.au
Website: www.imagespublishinggroup.com

National Library of Australia
Cataloguing-in-Publication Data

Cool Architecture

ISBN: 1 920744 27 4

1. Building—design and construction—climate factors—pictorial works.
2. Architecture and climate.
3. Architecture—20th century.

720.47

Coordinating Editor: Sarah Noal
Designed by The Graphic Images Studio Pty Ltd, Mulgrave, Australia
Film separations by SC (Sang Choy) International Pte Ltd.
Printed by Max Production Printing & Book-binding Limited

IMAGES has included on its website a page for special notices
in relation to this and our other publications. It includes updates
in relation to the information printed in our books. Please visit
this site: www.imagespublishinggroup.com

Contents

12–15   Administration Building for the Governor
         of Svalbard
             Jarmund/Vigsnæs AS Architects MNAL

16–19   The Alaska Public Health Laboratory and Office
         of the State Medical Examiner
             Livingston Slone, Inc.

20–23   Alaska Sealife Center
             Livingston Slone, Inc. and Cambridge Seven
             Associates, Inc.

24–29   Are Sensus House
             Parviainen Architects Ltd

30–31   Biesse-Baenie Landmark
             Wingårdh Arkitektkontor AB

32–35   Denver International Airport Passenger Terminal
             Fentress Bradburn Architects

36–37   Floating Sauna
             Architectural Office of Casagrande & Rintala

38–41   Gerstein Science Information Centre—Morrison
         Pavilion
             Diamond and Schmitt Architects Incorporated

42–45   Hallenstein Apartments
             Avery Team Architecture Ltd

46–49   Hanamaki Municipal Gymnasium
             Furuichi & Associates

50–53   Helsinki Railway Station Platform Roofing
             Arkkitehtitoimisto Esa Piironen OY

54–59   Hotel in Patagonia
             Germán Del Sol

60–63   Hotham Heights Lodges
             Fooks Martin Sandow Anson

64–67   House in Vilnius
             S. Kuncevičius Architectural Office

68–71 Kita-Aizu Town Hall
Furuichi & Associates

72–73 La Vogealle Mountain Shelter
Architecture Studio

74–77 Maniilaq Health Center [IHS Replacement Hospital]
Livingston Slone, Inc. with Stone Marricini
and Patterson

78–81 Marriot Library Expansion, University of Utah
Gunnar Birkerts Associates
Carrier, Johnson, Wu Architects (Architects of Record)

82–85 Middlebury College Bicentennial Hall
Payette Associates, Inc.

86–91 Mike's House
Blue Sky Architecture

92–97 Mitchell Residence
Poss Architecture + Planning

98–103 National Museum of Wildlife Art
Fentress Bradburn Architects

104–109 Niesen Mountain House Addition and Renovation
Aebi & Vincent Architects SIA AG

110–111 Nötstäter Conference & Sea Resort
Wingårdh Arkitektkontor AB

112–113 Occidental Chemical Center
Cannon Design

114–115 The Olympic Hall
Niels Torp AS Arkitekter MNAL

116–119 Private Residence
Dubbe-Moulder Architects

120–121 Rafferty House
Alfredo De Vido

122–127 The Red House
Jarmund/Vigsnæs AS Architects MNAL

128–129 Résidence Levésque
Croft Pelletier Architectes

130–133 Sámı Lapp Museum & Northern Lapland
Visitor Center
Arkkitehtitoimisto Juhani Pallasmaa KY

134–137 Sanga-Säby Courses & Conferences, Hotel Annex
Hans Murman Arkitektkontor

138–141 Sastrugi Lodge
Dawson Brown Architecture

142–147 Sibelius Hall
Artto Palo Rossi Tikka Architects

148–153 Ski Lodge
Hans Murman Arkitektkontor

154–159 Smaralınd Shopping Centre
Building Design Partnership and ASK Arkitektar
(Iceland)

160–163 Snowboarders' Cottage
Ivan Kroupa Architects

164–167 Snow King Inn
Alfredo De Vido

168–173 Turtagrø Hotel
Jarmund/Vigsnæs AS Architects MNAL

174–177 Twin Mountain Bed and Breakfast Lodge
Dubbe-Moulder Architects

178–183 Villa on Lake Kalvıaı
Vilius Ir Partneriai Architectural Bureau

184–187 Villa von Bagh
Juhani Katainen Architects

188–191 Weathering Steel House
Shim-Sutcliffe Architects

Introduction

Some time ago The Images Publishing Group recognized a need to make cold-climate design more accessible to a wider readership. Although this area of architecture is specialized in meeting the requirements and constraints of particular climatic conditions, it is also a vital design practice undertaken in numerous countries around the globe. As depicted in the broad selection of work featured here, cold-climate design projects are located as far afield as Chile, North America, Scandinavia, Japan, and New Zealand, experiencing temperatures ranging from cold to extreme sub-zero.

In this unique publication, many intriguing cold-climate design issues are raised, encompassing everything from site orientation to building design and materials. Some projects focus more on the practical aspects of cold-climate design, while others concentrate on aesthetics but they all contribute to an insightful look at this important field of architecture. Each work demonstrates the architect's skilled and innovative approach to the challenge of cold-climate design in often fragile or hostile natural environments.

Projects

The administration building is situated at 78° north on Spitsbergen, an archipelago located approximately 352 miles (566.5 kilometers) north of Norway. This group of islands is also known by Norwegians as Svalbard or 'The Land with Cold Coasts,' as temperatures may often fall to between -4°F (-20°C) and -22°F (-30°C) for long periods throughout winter.

The project is a multipurpose building which contains housing, office areas, a library, garaging for snow scooters, and even a prison cell, among other functions, servicing the archipelago's approximately 2500-strong population. The architects' aim was to imply industrial building traditions (coal mining has a long-standing history in this area), while taking into consideration the special climatic conditions of the archipelago.

2

1   Wooden screen provides
an artificially lit landscape
throughout dark season

2   Glass wall opens lobby
toward landscape

3&4   Zinc 'skin' protects building
against harsh climate

The building is founded on an existing concrete construction left undamaged after a fire in which the old headquarters was burnt down. A new geometry for the building's 'hull' was devised so that its surface area could be increased without having to establish too many new structural pillars, which are very expensive to install because of the area's permafrost.

Both physical and mental 'protection' were important issues in the design strategy for the building's 'overcoat.' The zinc covering of both the building's walls and roof are equal in order to combat strong prevailing winds, which buffet the building and which also increase the wind-chill factor. The sharp-angled planes of this zinc cladding also mirror the swiftly changing light and weather conditions in the arctic region. The area experiences midnight sun from April to August, but from October to February, the sun lies under the horizon. The building's walls and overhanging roof are also angled to protect entrance areas from both snow and wind.

continued

5

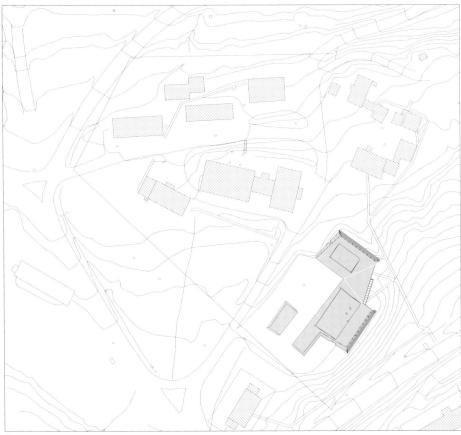

6

In front of the office windows, an open wooden screen gives shelter and provides an artificially lighted view from the office windows throughout the dark season; the artificial light is reflected by the snow and ice on the screens. The windows are covered with triple-layered glass filled with argon gas for maximum insulation because the temperature can range from 68°F (20°C) during summer to as low as (-58°F) -50°C during winter.

7

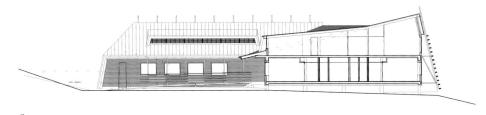

8

9   10

5   Roof landscape
6   Site plan
7   Southeast section
8   Triple-layered glass window
    filled with argon glass for
    optimal energy efficiency

9&10   Lobby
11   First floor plan
12   Ground floor plan
Photography:
    courtesy Jarmund/Vigsnæs AS
    Architects MNAL

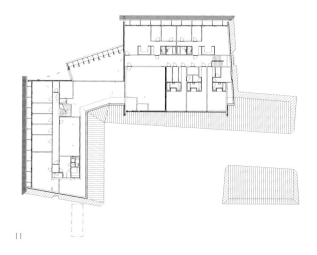

11

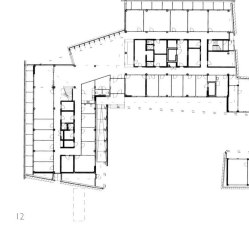

12

An aesthetic design goal for this metal- and glass-clad building was to be a 'center of scientific excellence,' and a place that says 'science is at work here.'

Due to the short amount of daylight during Alaska's winters, the introduction of natural light and views into many working spaces was very important. The office spaces were designed with large windows allowing natural light and outdoor views.

To prevent glare and provide diffused light, the design for upper windows in the office area included a custom-specified baked-on frit. This enables filtered light to enter without the glare typically caused by Alaska's low-angled sunlight.

Interior laboratories were designed to allow indirect light to pass through intervening spaces, giving laboratory staff the benefits of sunlight and outdoor views. The low

1 Tipped parapet reflects snow
   onto entry walk
2 Parking area and main entrance
   to laboratory

sun angles also gave opportunities for clerestories with special artistic glazing. The building was designed to glow with light reflected from the working areas onto the snow, providing a welcome to visitors.

Because this is a public building, energy efficiency was extremely important. Typically, in this cold climate, large convectors or 'radiators' are needed to overcome heat loss in laboratory spaces. Proper housekeeping of these large conventional units is difficult and they take up valuable floor space. To overcome these issues, subfloor radiant heating units were chosen. All mechanical systems are fully enclosed and easily accessible from indoors during inclement weather. The roof is flat and built to withstand snow loads and to prevent snow shed from damaging adjacent property or injuring people.

continued

3

The building is located adjacent to a wetlands area. In spring, winter snow melts from the parking areas, leading to higher than normal concentrations of tar and hydrocarbons. An ingenious planting of hardy plants adjacent to the roads and parking areas provides a biofiltration system to naturally clean the runoff before it reaches the critical wetlands habitat. Native plants were used throughout for a more natural landscaping and special moose-retardant screens were placed around the young trees.

4

3 Mechanical penthouses enclose laboratory
  ventilation equipment
4 Arctic vestibule with insulated translucent roof
5 Clerestory admits low midday sunlight
6 Brise soleil office area bounces light into
  laboratory on left
7 Clerestory artwork takes advantage of low sun
Photography: Chris Arend

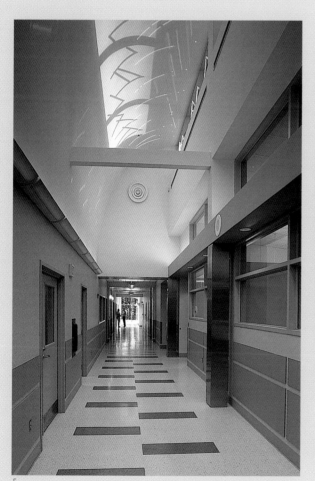

5

6

7

Alaska SeaLife Center

LIVINGSTON SLONE, INC. AND CAMBRIDGE SEVEN ASSOCIATES, INC.
Seward, Alaska, USA

The Alaska SeaLife Center, located in downtown Seward on Resurrection Bay, is committed to preserving the marine life of Alaska's coastal waters through research, rehabilitation, and education. In collaboration, Livingston Slone Architects and Cambridge Seven Associates worked closely with the Seward Association for the Advancement of Marine Science to develop the unique schematic design for the new center. Livingston Slone continued through final design and construction.

Sited adjacent to the University of Alaska's School of Fisheries and Ocean Sciences, one of the nation's top 10 centers for research on sub-arctic fish and invertebrates, the center attracts scientists from around the world interested in using the state-of-the-art facilities to study northern latitude species. The SeaLife Center is open year-round for visitors and researchers.

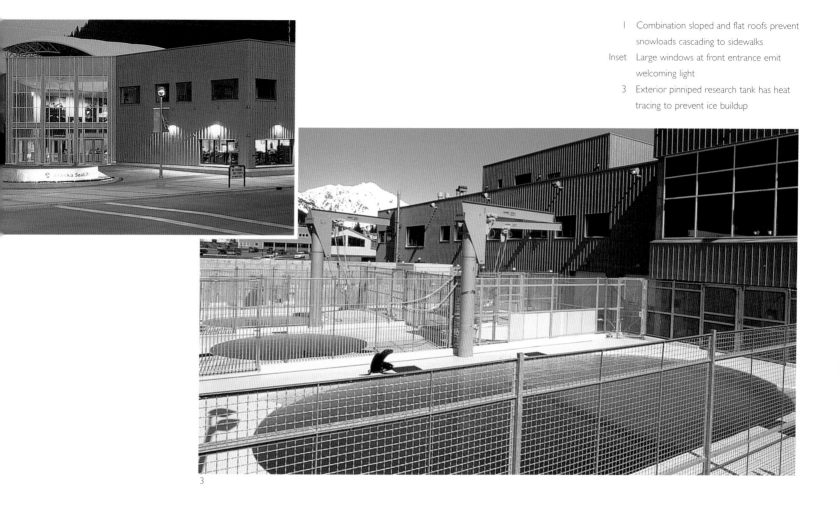

1 Combination sloped and flat roofs prevent snowloads cascading to sidewalks

Inset Large windows at front entrance emit welcoming light

3 Exterior pinniped research tank has heat tracing to prevent ice buildup

3

High wind conditions, as well as freezing rain, sleet, and heavy snowfall prevail in Seward's fall, winter, and early spring seasons. Flat roofs combined with a gently curved roofline over the aviary are designed to take large snow loads, and keep them from cascading down to cause property damage or injuries to pedestrians below. Other safety features included heated sidewalks to prevent treacherous ice from forming at the public entrance to the SeaLife Center. Heat tracing was included around the working tanks, within the accessible habitat rockwork and at the outdoor tank observation areas to prevent accidents due to slipping on ice. Heated floors keep all doors to the public observation areas from freezing closed or opened.

In similar facilities located in more temperate climes, a screen netting is used to contain birds in outdoor aviaries. In this northern location, Livingston Slone developed a solid, tent covering as driven sleet, rain and ice would have collected in the netting, ripping and collapsing the net in short order.

continued 21

Two materials dominate the exterior—concrete and zinc. Cast-in-place concrete was chosen for resistance to corrosion from wind-blown seawater, as well as the corrosive effects of marine research water circulation inside the facility. The unpainted zinc cladding on the building resists saltwater, weathers naturally, and requires no maintenance.

4   Tensioned fabric over steel frame
    covering bird aviary
5   Front entrance lobby windows
    afford spectacular views
6   Glass enclosures protect visitors
    from cold winds

Photography: Chris Arend

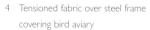

Are Sensus House, the new headquarters of Are Group, is located in Vantaa, in Helsinki Metro area. The project was completed in 2001 and accommodates an area of 80,730 square feet (7500 square meters).

The building consists of two long office 'vessels,' with a glass-roofed atrium that serves as a modifiable multipurpose space between them. During the cold winter months the light-filled atrium also functions as a general courtyard. The two-story-high atrium is surrounded by office areas, which form a visually and functionally uniform working community. The ground floor contains a semi-warm parking facility for 50 cars, a sauna, and a gym for personnel.

Sensus House has a compact layout to minimize the outside wall area and thus the loss of heat during winter, when temperatures can drop to around -22°F (-30ºC).

I   Main entrance to
Are Senus House

However, the layout and large glazed façades provide as much daylight as possible into workspaces throughout the long dark winters.

In Helsinki, while the temperature can drop to -22°F (-30°C) in winter it can also soar to 86°F (30°C) in summer. This means that in spring and autumn a problem often occurs. On the building's south side workspaces need to be cooled down while the other side of the building still needs to be heated. To accommodate this heating/cooling issue, Sensus House is equipped with an intelligent Ion-based Are-Sensus Hevac system that adjusts superbly to such variable temperatures.

The building is constructed from a concrete composite steel frame and hollow-core concrete slabs. The solid parts of the external walls are built on light-weight thermo purlin elements. The glazed façade sections are system glass walls realized with triple-insulation glass elements, mounted on an insulated steel and aluminum frame.

continued

2

3

4

2 Sun-protection grid on
   south elevation
3 Light pylons at main entrance
4 Library area in the office wing
Opposite Seating area on atrium mezzanine

The vivid metallic blue color of the cassette façades changes depending on the amount of light they receive, as well as the light's changing direction throughout the day's cycle and the different seasons experienced in the northern hemisphere.

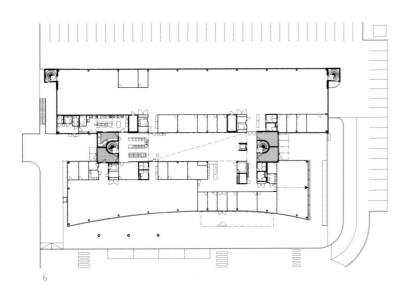

6

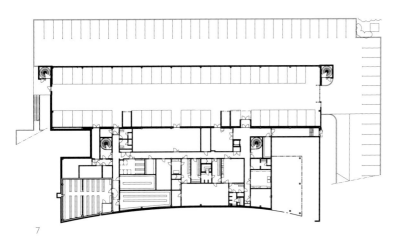

7

8

6   First floor plan
7   Ground floor plan
8   Atrium between office wings
9   Office room
10 Atrium seen from second-floor
    seating area
11 Second floor plan
12 Conference room interior

Photography: Voitto Niemelä

10

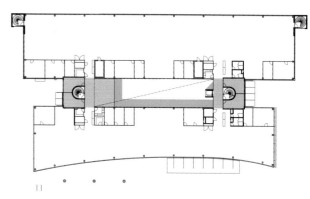

11

9

12

Biesse-Baenie Landmark

WINGÅRDH ARKITEKTKONTOR AB ■ Mount Östberget, Östersund, Sweden

Located on the summit of Mount Östberget, Östersund in northern Sweden, this unique project is designed to be a multifunctional landmark.

Biesse-baenie will act as both an arena and a meeting place, a symbolic connection of Östersund's past and future with the rest of Europe, and a place for reflection and meditation or peaceful activity. It will accommodate a hall which can seat up to 4000 people; a 'wisdom academy;' a Samic center about the people of Lapland; and a space for exhibitions and activities open to the public.

A wide roof will span the building's five major spaces or 'peaks.' These glass structures are designed to resemble a bear's teeth (after which the landmark is named) and their shapes also reflect the surrounding mountain topography.

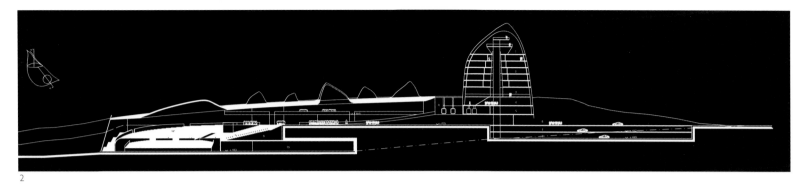

2

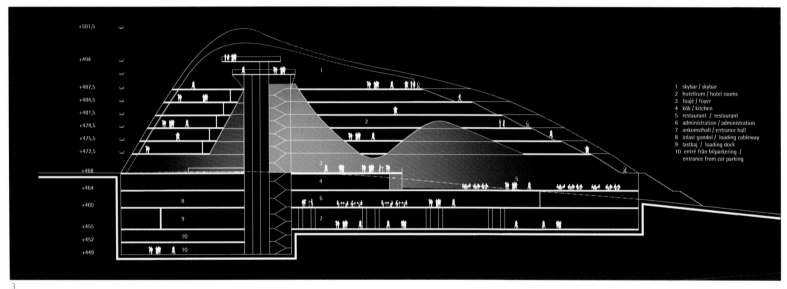

+501,5	
+494	
+487,5	
+484,5	
+481,5	
+478,5	
+475,5	
+472,5	
+468	
+464	
+460	8
+455	9
+452	10
+449	10

1 skybar / skybar
2 hotellrum / hotel rooms
3 foajé / foyer
4 kök / kitchen
5 restaurant / restaurant
6 administration / administration
7 ankomsthall / entrance hall
8 inlast gondol / loading cableway
9 lastkaj / loading dock
10 entré från bilparkering /
    entrance from car parking

3

The predominantly glass construction will be situated on the mountain's natural slopes and much of it will be submerged to blend with the surrounding landscape and to connect two ski slopes. The roof will be covered in grass and vegetation to further merge with its natural environment. In winter, the building will provide a snowy departure point for the mountain's extensive ski area.

The highest glass 'peak' houses a 200-room hotel for this ski destination, with expansive views of the surrounding landscape. At the time of publication, this project was underway.

1 Mount Österberget with the
   landmark hotel as its 'peak'

2 Section through auditorium,
   foyer, and cablecar

3 Section through hotel and two
   interior glazed courtyards

The soaring 'snow-capped peaks' of Denver International Airport's passenger terminal were inspired by the jagged profile of the nearby Rocky Mountains. But snow itself became a serious issue when officials first pondered the airport's design and wondered if the unique fabric roof could handle a serious snowfall.

To carry snow loads, the structure had to be properly shaped, engineered, and subjected to rigorous testing. A scale model of the terminal was studied in wind tunnel and water flume test chambers to simulate the actual wind and snow loads that could be expected on the new terminal roof. This process helped validate the expressive slopes and curvatures of the structure. Ultimately, the roof was engineered to withstand four times the amount of expected snow loads.

The 380,000-square-foot (35,300-square-meter) surface of the tensile membrane roof is stretched over 34 masts that stand as high as 120 feet (about 36.6 meters). The roof

2

Direct Light
Diffused Light
Refracted Light
Direct View of Sky

4

is reinforced with cables, of which half connect the pairs of masts and half run parallel to them across the 'valleys' between the masts. The mast cables, which look like the main cable of a suspension bridge, hold the structure up and carry downward loads, such as snow. The 'valley' cables, which take the form of an arch bridge, hold the structure down and resist upward loads, like wind. The roof itself is weightless and its components have no rigidity. Relying on curvature and tensile stress for stability, the roof is very pliable and

continued

1   Approach road meets curbside canopies on eastern façade
     Photography: Nick Merrick/Hedrich-Blessing
2   Canopies frame the south glass curtainwall
     Photography: Ron Johnson
Inset Design was inspired by profile of nearby Rocky Mountains
     Photography: Ellen Jaskol
4   Daylighting diagram

5

flexes under the impact of such upward and downward loads, like a tree or a spider's web.

The roof sheds snow through a combination of the waterproof skin and the arching curve of the valleys, which allows snow to slide and water to drain out onto lower roof areas. The protective overhangs over glass walls and the absence of conventional joints prevent leakage and reduce maintenance. In addition, the airport has reaped significant energy savings because of the great amount of daylight that permeates the translucent roof.

6

7

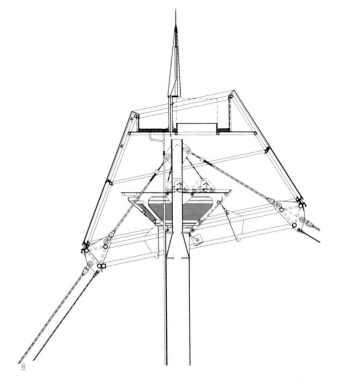

8

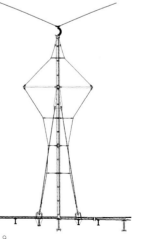

9

5 'Peaks' with skylights, from
   curbside, at sunset
   Photography: Nick Merrick/
   Hedrich-Blessing

6 Cables are contained within
   seams that curve up the side
   of the 'peaks'
   Photography: Ron Johnson

7 Interior is lit largely by daylight
   that penetrates translucent roof
   Photography: Nick Merrick/
   Hedrich-Blessing

8 Mast top longitudinal section

9 South wall cable truss section

This floating sauna was designed as a prototype in a workshop with Västlands Kunstakademie, Bergen, and then donated to the residents of Rosendal Village in Norway. It offers a welcome retreat for physical and mental relaxation interspersed with invigorating swims in Hardangerfjord.

Anchored in the middle of the fjord, the sauna's location ensures that bathers can maintain a sense of privacy. The sauna is 269.1 square feet (25 square meters) and constructed from pine with plastic walls, which admit a limited amount of light. Inside, to heat the sauna, stones are warmed on a Norwegian Jötul-oven. When bathers wish to cool down, they simply jump into the lake below formed by a hole in the sauna's floor.

2

3

1&4   Sauna interior featuring
      Norwegian Jötul-oven and
      plunge pool
   2   Floating sauna is anchored in
      Norway's Hardangerfjord
   3   Sauna's plastic walls admit
      natural light
Photography: Sami Rintala

4

Due to a warm gulf stream around the west coast of Norway, where the fjord is located, the surrounding sea and fjord do not freeze over in winter. This means that the sauna remains accessible by boat and in use during winter. The interior temperature may be 86°F (90°C) while the temperature outside can be as low as -4°F (-20°C).

The University of Toronto retained Diamond and Schmitt Architects Incorporated to develop a master plan and initiate a multi-phased renovation of the Gerstein Science Information Centre on the St. George campus. As well as the interior renovation and restoration of the existing Sigmund Samuel building, a new addition was built. This created 40 percent more stack space and 30 percent more reader space with only an 8-percent increase in area. The new 31,000-square-foot (2880-square-meter) Morrison Pavilion was completed in 2002.

A goal of the new design was to bring the student work stations as close to the exterior light and views as possible. In Toronto, the majority of the school year occurs in winter with limited daylight and dreary conditions, so it was important to use as much

2

1 View looking south
2 View of surrounding University
   of Toronto campus
Photography: Steven Evans

natural light as possible. To achieve this, the design included large bay windows, the views from which overlook an attractive landscape and an array of historical buildings.

The size of the windows at the building's edges was also maximized to compensate for the pavilion's large book-stack floor plate. However, the large windows, while letting in more light, meant that the effects of glare on computer screens needed to be controlled. The design began with careful analysis of the sun angles on the east-facing elevation of the building. Then a combination of ceramic frit screening and slightly tinted glass was used to control the direct glare of the sun. *continued*

3

4

Another issue with the expansive glazing was the effects of Toronto's climate shifts from extremes of -4°F (–20°C) in winter to 95°F (35°C) in summer, and the need to maintain a stable temperature for the student study spaces. A strategy of exposed mechanical ductwork allows tempered air to be delivered as close as possible to the workstations. Freestanding radiant heating is also located at the perimeter glazing to accommodate heating requirements in the winter months.

3   Detail of windows
4   Pavilion window detail
5   View looking northwest
Inset   East elevation

Photography: Steven Evans

1

2

1 Street view
  Photography: Johannes Van Kan

2 Entry to Apartment 1
  Photography: Craig Muir

3 View over Lake Whakatipu
  from Apartment 1 terrace
  Photography: Johannes Van Kan

Located close to the Southern Alps on New Zealand's South Island, Queenstown is a popular skiing and recreational center. Winter temperatures do not drop as low as those of the nearby mountain ski resorts, but they do frequently nudge freezing point.

The client's brief for this project was to create apartments with an alpine character using natural local materials. It was also important to maximize the views from the site

high above Queenstown, to the town, the lake, and mountains beyond. The same theme is carried through to the interiors, to create a refined yet warm and inviting atmosphere.

The site's topography proved challenging with a 65.6-foot (20-meter) fall over its 180.4-foot (55-meter) length. However, the desired 180-degree-views were found

continued

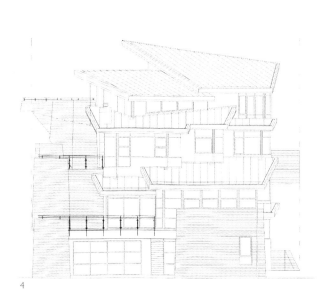

4

5

6

over the upper 82 feet (25 meters) of the site—and the resulting best location for the house. The building straddles the slope over five stories of predominantly masonry construction in front of a 29.5-foot-high (9-meters) soil-nailed stabilized retaining wall.

Conceptually, the building is a number of discreet elements, comprising massive schist buttresses, a series of interlocking glazed and timber volumes, capped with floating zinc roof planes. The stone buttress walls visually anchor the house into the site's steep slope. The zinc roof blends into the hillside and reduces glare from lower roofs when viewed from the floors above.

The integration of indoor and outdoor areas was a high priority, and the flow of space from the living areas onto the protected northwest oriented terraces was carefully considered. Bi-folding doors open the upper house living area onto a dark heat-absorbing granite-surfaced terrace.

Other design considerations for the location's climate include energy-efficient, double-glazed windows. Motorized louvers to the glazing over the upper apartment stairway were installed on the north elevation to provide solar shading in summer and to allow the sun to penetrate deep into the house in winter.

Insulated concrete block walls, under-floor heating, and granite-clad gas fireplaces also ensure warm living after a day on the slopes.

4 Southwest elevation

5 Apartment 1 dining

6 Apartment 1 hallway

7 Main approach at night
   Photography: Johannes Van Kan

8 Long section

9 Second floor plan

10 Living area
   Photography: Johannes Van Kan

11 Ensuite
   Photography: Craig Muir

12 First floor plan

7

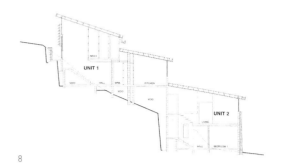

8

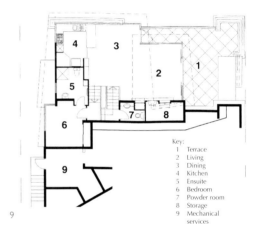

Key:
1 Terrace
2 Living
3 Dining
4 Kitchen
5 Ensuite
6 Bedroom
7 Powder room
8 Storage
9 Mechanical
   services

9

Key:
1 Entry
2 Garage
3 Motorcourt
4 Storage
5 Void
6 Mud room
7 Hall
8 Bathroom
9 Bedroom

10

11

12

Hanamaki City is located in northeastern Japan—an area that can experience heavy snowfall in winter. Traditional Japanese houses are wooden with pitched roofs to allow for snow slide-off and to prevent roof damage from the weight of heavy snow loads. However, this can be risky if snow slides onto unsuspecting passersby. Also, residents must then clear the fallen snow from roofs, away from building entrances and accesses.

For this reason, Furuichi & Associates adopted a different roof type for the gymnasium. With its waveform design and lightweight structure reinforced with steel frames, this roof is able to withstand heavy snow loads. Such a design concept means that snow remains on the roof until it is either blown off by strong winter winds or melts in spring. The building was also oriented to maximize on the roof's exposure to these seasonal winds so that piling snow is blown off it regularly.

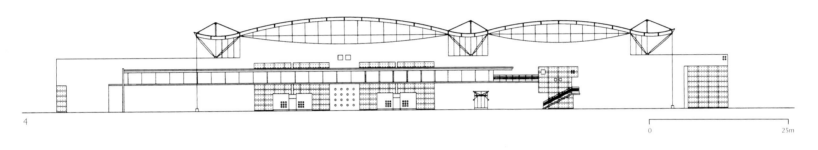

4

0   25m

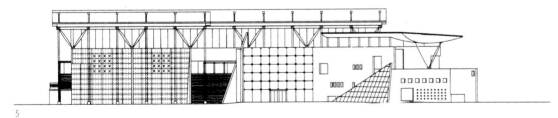

5

The gymnasium's interior design is also considerate of the building's location and harsh winter climate. As much natural light as possible permeates the gymnasium's interior through elongated windows which complement the building's roof design. Natural light even enhances the gymnasium's artificial lighting on dull winter days.

As a municipal building open to the public, the gymnasium's glass entrance hall also provides a warm welcome. For its design, the vertical loads are suspended from the roof of the building, supported by arched horizontal tension beams to combat high-velocity winds and occasional seismic activity. Condensation forming on the glass surfaces, from winter drafts at the entrance doors is dispelled by the use of warm-air vents in the ceiling.

Other practical considerations for using the gymnasium during winter include an undercover running track. This wraps around the outside wall of the gymnasium building for public use in winter when the ground is snow covered.

6

7

8

6　Entrance hall interior

7　Entrance plaza

8　Interior view of entrance's glass façade

9　Indoor running track with outdoor view

10　Sports hall

Photography: Osamu Murai

11　First floor plan

12　Second floor plan

9

10

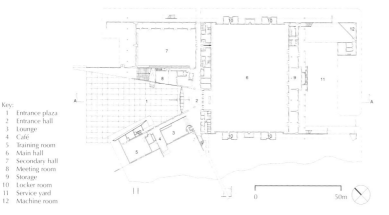

Key:
1　Entrance plaza
2　Entrance hall
3　Lounge
4　Café
5　Training room
6　Main hall
7　Secondary hall
8　Meeting room
9　Storage
10　Locker room
11　Service yard
12　Machine room

11

0　　　　　　　　50m

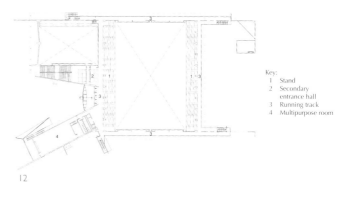

Key:
1　Stand
2　Secondary
　　entrance hall
3　Running track
4　Multipurpose room

12

1

2

The Helsinki railway station was built in 1919 by architect Eliel Saarinen. At the time, he designed three different roofing plans for the station but none of them was realized. The project plan for the platform roofing is based on the winning entry of an architectural competition. The roof design was then further developed to meet the client's wishes.

It was important that the new roofing system should remain respectful of Saarinen's existing buildings, while also providing modern and practical platform shelters. During winter, Helsinki experiences short daylight hours so the roof of the station hall and the roof and walls of each platform shelter are made of glass. This design provides as much daylight as possible to the station's customers and to the interior of the original premises.

3

4

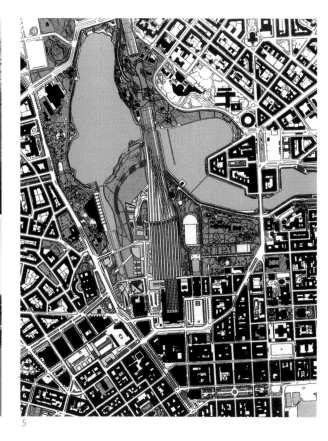

5

The dimensions of the roofing system are largely dependent on the existing station building. The 172.2-by-742.7-square-foot (16-by-69-square-meter) end-platform shelter over the main platform area in the southern section adjoins the station hall. The shelter over platforms 4 to 11 is 541.3 feet long (165 meters) and serves most of the passengers of the long-distance trains and some of the commuting trains. The state-of-the-art high-speed Pendolino train fits completely under the platform shelter.

continued

51

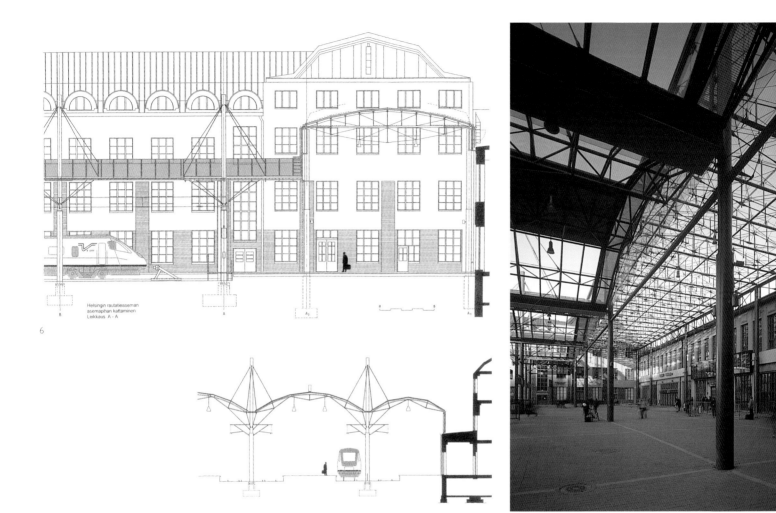

6

Helsingin rautatieaseman
asemapihan kattaminen
Leikkaus A - A

7

8

The glass shelters look deceptively light but they have been reinforced by load-bearing steel frame structures. In addition, the end-platform shelter is built on steel piles and the columns by the walls are mounted on pilasters injected into the concrete wall of the station building.

Helsinki experiences sub-zero temperatures during winter, to around -22°F (-30°C) at times, and summer temperatures have been known to rise to about 86°F or (30°C). Rainfall and snow are also common so a solid roof structure was essential for safety and to protect commuters from diverse weather conditions.

The roof design also takes into account considerable rainfall. Water runs from beside the roof's frame columns into a rainwater system. Drainage is also centralized at track level between the trains, allowing rainwater to run off into the track's gravel layer.

10

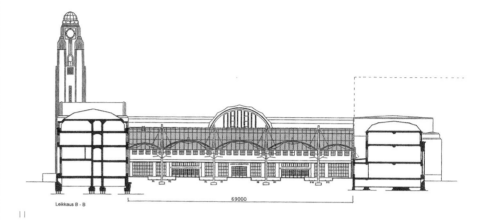

Leikkaus B - B   69000

11

12

6 Section

7 Section

8 Modern glazed roof structure does not detract from
   building's original architecture
   Photography: Jussi Tianen

9 Roofing's suspended steel truss construction
   Photography: Esa Piironen

10 Glazed roof admits extensive natural light to interior
    Photography: Jussi Tianen

11 Section

12 Platform shelter's steel frame structure
    Photography:Esa Piironen

This hotel was designed to provide accommodation for visitors to the remote southernmost regions of Chile. Located on the banks of Lake Pehoé, the hotel lies in the 500,000-acre wilderness of the Torres del Paine National Park, which is fringed with ice fields to the south.

The weather conditions here can change rapidly from sun to rain to snow and the area is often exposed to strong northerly winds. During summer months, the temperature can rise to around 82.4°F (28°C), dropping to 23°F (-5°C) at night. Throughout winter, the temperature may fall to about 10.4°F (-12°C).

As a result, special consideration was given to the building materials used for the hotel. A waterproof membrane envelops not only the roof but also the building's façades to protect against driving rain and snow. Materials also needed to be elastic

54

2

1　Walkway leading to and
　　from hotel

2　Hotel's low-lying form remains
　　unobtrusive in its surroundings

3　Glaciers run from the southern
　　ice fields to Chilean Patagonia

enough to adapt to the dramatically changing weather conditions and to be especially resistant to material fatigue, which such climatic changes can cause.

To combat strong prevailing winds, the building has an aerodynamic form, so that wind can stream past the hotel without undue pressure being placed on its extensive glazing. These large and prominent windows afford stunning views of the surrounding landscape and ensure ample natural lighting to the hotel's interior.

Torres del Paine National Park is part of the United Nation's World Biosphere Reserve system, to be protected and enjoyed. Therefore, the architect was faced with the dual challenge to always remain sensitive to the hotel's unique environment while running a safe and functional hotel in such a remote area.

The hotel is a low-lying form designed so that it is not glimpsed at first sight and never dominates the landscape. It accommodates up to 60 visitors in 28 double rooms and two

continued

5

6

4

7

8

suites. A reception, lounge, bar, and restaurant in a single open-plan area are on the ground level, with a games room downstairs. Outside, a walkway leads down to an indoor swimming pool, massage room and sauna, and adjacent outdoor Jacuzzis.

4   Hotel's white 'plank' exterior reflects ever-changing skies

5   Warm interior shelters hotel guests from frozen landscape

6   Hotel is located in the remote Torres del Paine National Park

7   Hotel at night

8   Dining room enjoys spectacular views

9   Heated indoor pool with multiple windows and skylights

10 Hotel rooms are positioned to maximize views

11

12

13

14

15

11 Stair to dining room
12 Comfortable seating areas with
     extensive glazing
13 Fireplaces are located in public
     areas throughout hotel
14 Detail of wood finish
15 Wood finish provides kaleidoscope
     of color
16 Subtle lighting enhances warmth
     of interior
17 Intimate gathering spaces accentuate
     relaxed hotel environment
18 Hotel bar

Photography: Guy Wenborne

16

17

18

Hotham Heights Lodges

FOOKS MARTIN SANDOW ANSON ■ Mount Hotham, Victoria, Australia

Mount Hotham is home to a popular ski resort in the heart of the Victorian Alps. The design brief was to develop the Basin site of the resort—a slope for beginner and intermediate skiers—into premier ski accommodation, in order to diversify the existing accommodation on offer.

The result is Hotham Heights Lodges, a series of three-story chalets grouped together on Basin slope and linked by a network of elevated walkways. The range of chalets

are specifically oriented to provide protection from harsh conditions while maintaining spectacular northern panoramic views. The site layout for the lodges also afforded real opportunities to maximize solar access and a multistory, cuboid building form was adopted to capitalize on thermal efficiency.

Careful management of snow dump was required to ensure site accessibility and safety for visitors and occupants. Roofs are pitched so that snow is directed into non-access areas, away from entrances and balconies. For easier vehicle access to the site, a concrete roadway is heated electrically to prevent hazardous driving

2

3

1 Views across to Mt. Loch
2 Vertical building forms assist
   in thermal efficiency
3 Interiors offer panoramic
   views

conditions. In addition, adjoining undercover parking offers a level of drive-in/drive-out amenity unique to the Hotham resort.

The lodges' exteriors feature a variety of cladding from traditional alpine timbers to galvanized metal sheeting ruled with vertically expressed ribs for durability. Radial-cut stringy bark is used not only for the visual effect of irregular linear pattern, but also for its hardy performance in the strong cycles of wet and dry, hot and cold, which can erode the most resilient of materials.

Inside, architectural features are described in bold pigments against snow-white walls. Materials and textures are carefully coordinated to evoke a sense of warmth and relaxation. Cantilevered corner windows and areas of floor-to-ceiling glass provide a dramatic precipitous outlook into the valley below.

The Hotham Heights Village is now a developing community—a neighborhood of lodges strategically located on a spectacular site, each building having regard for its neighbor's presence. The emphasis on simplicity and function sets a design precedent for future development with a vision toward a year-round alpine experience.

5

6

Opposite: Hotham Heights village
offers visual diversity to
Hotham landscape

5   Vertical building forms
assist in thermal
efficiency

6   Elevated walkways
provide easy access

Photography: Peter Clarke

The nearly symmetrical L-shaped design of this house is reminiscent of a huge bird spreading its wings in flight. The project's layout and oblique façades, which taper to its roof, embody this metaphoric idea employed by the building's architects.

Materials for this house were chosen carefully to cope with Lithuania's colder weather. Throughout winter, the country regularly experiences sub-zero temperatures, averaging around 23°F (-5°C). Freeze-thaw cycles are frequent with strong prevailing winds from the Baltic coast, considerable precipitation, and freezing fog.

Wood, brick, and glass are the primary materials used for this project. The façades with horizontal paneling are of larch wood. Thermal insulation has been added to the home's wall and roof construction to minimize the heat flow between the internal

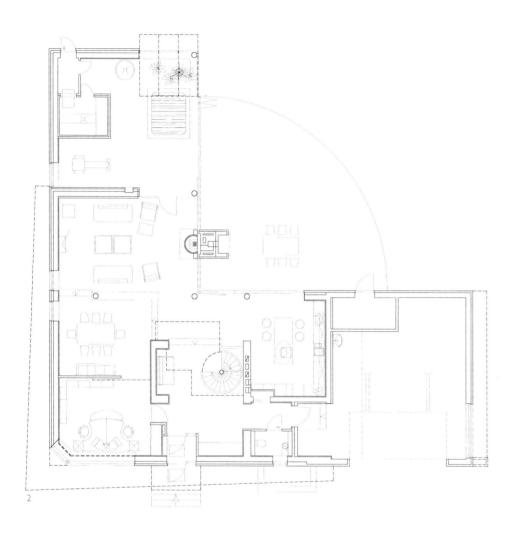

2

3

and external sides of the building. Harnessing thermal conductivity is particularly important in winter when the temperature inside the house might be 68°F (20°C) but it is freezing or below outside.

The house is also heated using a geothermic heat pump. Since 1994, Lithuania has used its shallow geothermal energy resources, which are the easiest to reach. This heating

continued

1 Main façade

2 Ground floor

3 Hall

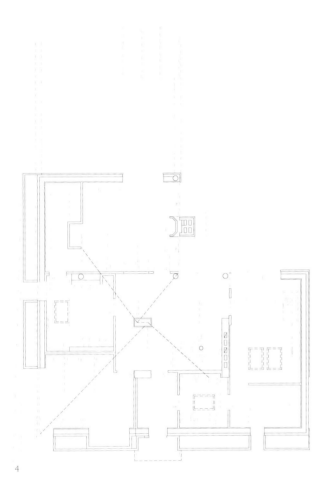

4

method requires heating tubes positioned on the ground so that they can heat both the floor and the air inside the house. The system is easy to run and cheap to install.

Glass windows have been placed selectively in this home, with wooden window frames on the interior—as a warm, comfortable material—but aluminum window frames externally to weather the cold climate. Façades with considerable glazing are oriented to the south and west for best day- and sunlighting, while the northern façade has few windows.

5

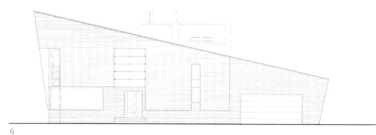

6

7

8

4   First floor
5   Living room
6   Elevation
7&8 Pool

Photography: Vytautas Širvinskas

The roof is pitched on a 15-degree incline, optimal for snow and rainwater drainage, and has only two gutters due to the risk of pipe blockage by pine needles falling from the surrounding trees. A typical Lithuanian cold-climate feature is the indoor porch. This is a small but important room in the house's design because it prevents the warm air inside from dispersing out of the home's entrance when the door is open.

In northern Japan, where this project is located, strong winds and snow frequently buffet buildings throughout the cold winter months. To shelter structures from such harsh weather conditions, hedges are often grown around them. However, for the Kita-Aizu Town Hall, a different solution was found.

A U-shaped concrete wall protects internal office space from northwesterly winds and snowstorms. The thickness of the wall was increased more than structurally necessary in order to minimize heat loss from the building and further insulation materials were also added. The interior floor plan complements the building's shielding design too, as any spaces adjacent to the concrete wall are not in constant use. These include meeting rooms, restrooms, stairs, elevators, storage, and printing rooms, providing another 'protecting layer' between the building's office space and its exterior.

2   3   4

Only a few windows punctuate the U-shaped wall for heat-loss prevention, while the south, less exposed side of the building is glazed to allow in ample natural light. Ceiling skylights above tall wood columns also admit natural light to the interior, and in the office area the high ceiling, which is supported by these columns, enhances the sense of space. The use of natural light contributes to significant energy savings because artificial light is not required during the day, even in winter. Equally, light and space are important for employees' general wellbeing during dull winter months.

To heat such a large, high-ceilinged space was not possible with an ordinary air-conditioning system, as warmed air would have remained in the upper part of the room. Instead, under-floor heating was added.

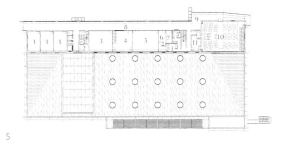

5

Key:
1   Committee room
2   Storage
3   Chairman's room
4   Office
5   Lobby
6   Library
7   Locker room
8   Corridor
9   Assembly hall
    lobby
10 Assembly hall
11 Committee
    waiting room

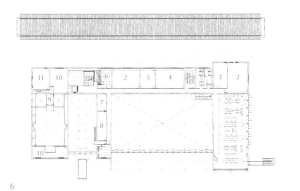

6

Key:
1   Office
2   Meeting room
3   Drafting room
4   Education Board
5   Head of
    Education Board
6   Rest area
7   Meeting room
8   Library
    (fire-resistant)
9   Lighting and
    sound room
10 Machine room
11 Storage

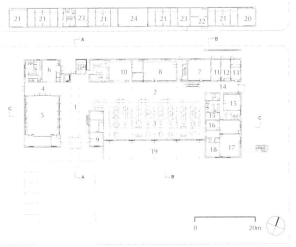

7

Key:
1   Entrance Hall
2   Lobby
3   Office
4   Small lobby
5   Main Hall
6   Lounge
7   Library
8   Meeting room
9   Consulting room
10 Office
11 Computer center
12 Press room
13 Guards' room
14 Staff entrance
15 Locker room
16 Mail room
17 Mayor's room
18 Reception room
19 Terrace
20 Parking lot
    (cycles)
21 Parking for
    officials
22 Machine control
    room
23 Electricity
    control
24 Storage

0   20m

8

9

10

11

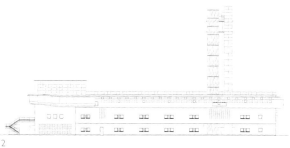

12

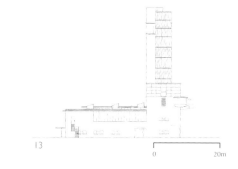

13

0   20m

14

5   Third floor plan
6   Second floor plan
7   First floor plan
8   Night view of entrance hall
9   Entrance hall interior
10 Wood canopy
11 Night view of office
12 North elevation
13 East elevation
14 Skylights illuminate office space

Photography: Osamu Murai

La Vogealle Mountain Shelter
ARCHITECTURE STUDIO ■ Samoëns, France

This project is located close to the alpine town of Sixt-Fer-à-Cheval—a popular ski resort in the Fer à Cheval natural reserve of the French Alps, which border Switzerland. This area, known as the Grand Massif, has some 155.3 miles (250km) of marked ski runs and also offers year-round alpine activities.

La Vogealle is situated overlooking the 'Valley of the Ends of the Earth' at 6562 feet (2000 meters) above sea level. In such a pristine landscape it is important that the building's architecture remains sympathetic to its natural surroundings and causes minimal damage to this protected habitat. Therefore, the structure will be set on stilt foundations to avoid modification to the natural site and to stabilize the shelter in such an exposed location.

The project will be built on the site of an existing chalet, the materials from which will be dismantled and recycled as far as possible for the new building's construction. Access to the site is via mountain roads linked to nearby towns. However, some building materials may need to transported to the site by helicopter, although the intention is to limit helicopter use in order to meet sustainable design requirements.

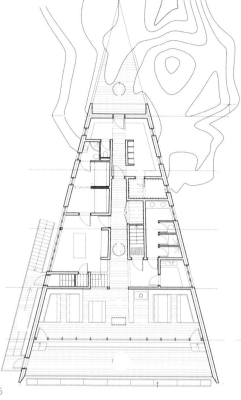

1 Side view featuring emergency exit
2 South-west facing glass façade
3 Rear view and panorama
4 Structural view
5 Floor plan

The mountainous surroundings and resulting extreme climatic conditions have influenced the project's architectural design in other ways too. For example, the traditional mountain chalet architecture of this region inspired the design of the building's dual-sloped steel and aluminum roof. The roof design's triangular geometry also reflects the form of the impressive Tenneverge Mountain ridge, which can be viewed from the shelter.

The shelter is positioned to maximize on its orientation to the sun in order to use solar power as a more ecologically sound energy source for the chalet. The building will accommodate up to 56 people, anticipated to be visitors to the region, such as trekkers and skiers. The chalet will be used both in summer and in winter, when stoves will be the interior's primary heat source.

Dominant winds are also a major factor for this location and building the house on 'stilts' will not only fix the structure to the site but also help to avoid snow build up around the chalet due to these strong winds.

For full enjoyment of the panoramic views from the chalet, the south-west façade of the chalet's common living space is entirely glazed.

The City of Kotzebue (population 3000) is located 30 miles (48.3 kilometers) above the Arctic Circle and is called the Gateway to Northwest Alaska. Kotzebue serves as a regional center for outlying villages and communities. This state-of-the-art medical facility, completed in 1998, services Kotzebue and the northwest region of the state. The hospital incorporates 17 acute care beds, three delivery rooms, a laboratory, radiology, emergency treatment areas, and large outpatient areas for dental, medical care, and counseling.

The 82,000-square-foot (7618-square-meter) facility is designed to withstand the rigors of a severe arctic climate. Like most buildings in Kotzebue, the hospital is elevated on pilings to prevent settlement due to melting permafrost. However, the clients wanted heated, ground-level entrances for optimum accessibility. Although only a one-story building, the under-floor and above-ceiling interstitial cavities add greatly to the center's bulk. To overcome the transition from grade to finish floor, massive entry structures were designed to accommodate patients, ambulance service, and freight.

2

3

1   At-grade entry points:
    penthouses for ventilation
    equipment
2   Large arctic entry vestibule
3   Front elevation shows raised
    thermo siphon piling

To ensure a solid foundation, the building rests on 400 passive thermo syphon piles set 20 feet (6.1 meters) into the permafrost soil to draw off excess heat. Except for the entranceway, free air space between the building's underside and grade prevents foundation failure from heat transfer and allows wind scour to reduce snowdrifts around the building. Rooftop mechanical systems are enclosed in slope-roofed penthouses, uniquely designed to allow the intake of outside air without ingesting large quantities of snow into the ventilation system.

The large, at-grade entries required that strict attention be paid to block the wind and snow from the interior of the building. The entry stairs and elevators are contained in large 'arctic entry' vestibules that take advantage of stratified air principles to enhance comfort and energy conservation. Inside the vestibules at the patient lobby, a full-height glazed windscreen and short walls further block and direct the cold wind. The walls and glass entries allow a feeling of spaciousness while conserving energy and protecting visitors and staff from cold arctic air.

continued

5

6

4 Glazed windscreen
   diverts arctic air
   from seating
5 Public lobby with
   glazed windscreen
   at inner door
6 Ground level of arctic
   entry vestibule
7 Waiting area: low wall
   diverts cold wind
8 Windows in hospital
   corridor afford staff
   outdoor views

Photography: Chris Arend

7

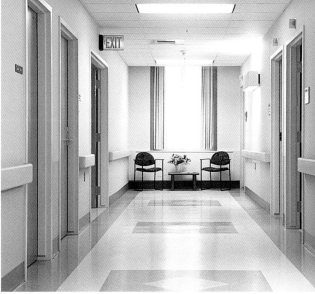

8

The short three-month outdoor building season dictated the assemblage of pre-made, high thermal value exterior panels for the roof, walls, and under-floor. This allowed rapid envelope enclosure before the onset of winter weather.

After careful analysis of the functional and urban conditions of the existing university campus, it was decided that the Marriot Library expansion would be located underground. The 207,000-square-foot (19,230-square-meter) library addition, surrounds the existing library on three sides and its two U-shaped floors align and connect with the original five-story library.

The new building is respectful of the overall campus character and landforms. It also offers a practical year-round study environment in a location where temperatures can drop to around -22°F (-30°C) during winter and soar to as much as 104°F (40°C) in summer. The addition houses several functions including the collections and readers stations of the Science and Engineering Division and the Circulation Services

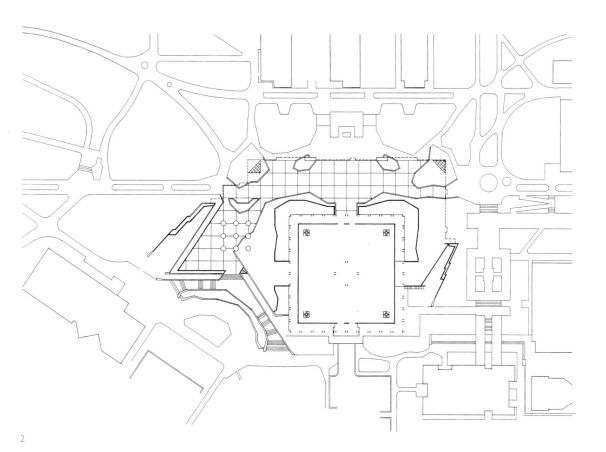

2

3

4

1   Stair transition to surface plaza
2   Site plan
3   Roof, campus circulation area
4   Light court in summer

Division. It also includes a general reserve, an assembly room, and an audio-visual/student computer center.

Because the addition is subterranean, its exterior exposure is limited to two-story-high light courts, the northwest entrance, and three skylight assemblies. The light courts are constructed of four-sided structural insulated glazing, using vision and spandrel glass, precast concrete, and aluminum louvers. The skylight assemblies are constructed from similar glazing using tinted or reflective glass. On both of the addition's two floors, the collections are located toward the buried perimeter, remote from daylight, while the reader stations are located adjacent to the light courts.

continued

5   Light court in summer

6   Stair transition to surface plaza

7   Roof, campus circulation area

8   Light court and skylight
     illuminate underground level

9   Entrance lobby

10 Skylights admit light to
     underground level

11 Control desk at lobby entrance

12 Second floor plan

13 First floor plan

Photography: Balthazar Korab

5

6

7

8

9

Fresh air intake and relief air and exhaust air are discharged through louvers in the walls. Because of constrained floor-to-floor and roof-to-floor heights, main distribution ducts are located under the first floor slab and connect to vertical shafts at the buried perimeter of the addition.

Overall, the campus planning concept works with two grids (north to south and northeast to southwest). Most buildings are oriented on the informal northeast-to-southwest grid but

10

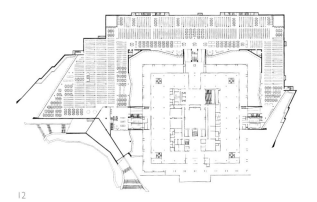

12

11

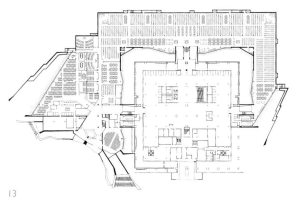

13

the addition follows the formal north-to-south grid. However, all the surface formations of hard walkways and courtyards are based on a free polygonal form development, enforcing an organic, less structured architecture. The roof of the structure is also covered with extensive lawn areas subject to snow cover in winter.

Middlebury College's Bicentennial Hall is located on a prominent ridge at the northwest corner of the campus with extensive views to the Adirondacks and the Green Mountains. Bicentennial Hall is a multidisciplinary academic building that houses all of the laboratory sciences at Middlebury. As the centrepiece of the college's 200th anniversary, the structure is considered one of the few landmark buildings on the campus. The exterior design utilises, in a distinctly progressive

manner, forms and materials that are familiar to the campus. The exterior envelope is extremely energy efficient and is expected to last beyond 100 years.

The walls and roof are thermally efficient and resistant to corrosion, ice dams, and water penetration. The Indiana and dolomitic limestone veneer is self-supporting (with minimal intermediate supports) to avoid the thermal bridging typical in traditional stone veneer support systems. Five inches (12.7 centimeters) of semi-rigid mineral

North Quad

3

1   East entry
    Photography: Jeff Goldberg/Esto
2   View from west
3   Site plan
4   Campus context
    Photography: Bob Handelman

2

4

wool insulation (fabricated by forming steel slag and basalt stone into a semi-rigid board material) was used instead of the industry standard, 2 inches or 5 centimeters of foam insulation, to avoid the use of ozone depleting HCFs or CFCs. Super-insulating, triple-glazed windows were also integrated into the building to provide 2.5 times more insulating value than typical high-quality, low e/argon glazing.

The tilt-up precast 'wall columns' (formed locally) allowed the contractor to achieve 75 percent enclosure during the Vermont winter before the stone veneer was installed. The slate roof utilizes a prototypal cold roof system with structural insulating panels and 3 inches (about 7.6 centimeters) of ventilation space, which allows air to travel underneath the roof to keep it cold, and eliminates ice dams and snow build-up.

continued

7

8

9

10

The central Great Hall is a vital campus resource, especially valuable in a cold climate. The extensive curtainwalls facing south and west provide desired warmth during much of the year. The Great Hall's conditioned air is supplied to the laboratories in order to save energy. The building's cruciform plan defines four distinct outdoor spaces including the Discovery Court, which is a popular meeting spot due to its southwest orientation. Furthermore, end-wall entrances on three of the building's wings allow students and faculty the opportunity to enter at the nearest possible point while avoiding snow slides from sloping roofs.

5   Discovery Court

Inset   East elevation

Photography: Jeff Goldberg/Esto

7   Façade detail

Photography: Jonas Kahn

8&9   Great Hall

10   View to west

11   Classroom

Photography: Jeff Goldberg/Esto

11

The site for this 3498-square-foot (325-square-meter) house is in the Coastal Mountains of Western Canada near Whistler Mountain. It is a varied topography including a beautiful outcrop of glaciated granite with great alpine views of Wedge Mountain to the east and the forest on the base of Rainbow Mountain to the west. Temperatures range from -22°F (–30°C) in January to 86°F (30°C) in August. Snowfall accumulations over 3 feet (about 1 meter) are possible.

The owner of the house is a naturalist with a strong environmental aesthetic. It was important that the house should fit into the natural landscape and have minimal impact on the site. The plan curves to embrace the granite outcrop, while the section was developed to straddle the granite on the east and drop below it toward the forest on the west.

2

3

4

The shed roofs rise in opposite slopes. A heavy timber post and beam structure defines a radial path through the house. Spaces have a gentle sense of movement, a comfortable scale, and are constructed of visually warm materials. The exposed timber structure and a large natural log column form the space and spirit of the house. The roof and east window-wall is a structural post and beam system that transfers the tremendous roof snow loads down to the

continued

1   East elevation and granite outcrop
    Photography: John Fulker

2   North elevation seen through winter trees
    Photography: Bo Heliwell

3   'Bird house' bedroom on north elevation
    Photography: John Fulker

4   East elevation in snow
    Photography: Leanna Rathkelly

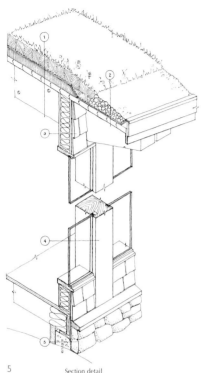

5

Section detail
1　Alpine grass and flower mix
　　Growing medium
　　Geotex filter cloth
　　Two ply torch-down membrane
　　100-millimeter ISO insulation board
　　Ice and water peel-and-stick membrane
　　65-millimeter fir t&g decking
　　Two 200- by 400-millimeter fir beams
2　Drain gravel at all edges
3　Interior wall finish
　　38- by 140-millimeter fir wall framing
　　140-millimeter glass fiber insulation
　　12.7-millimeter fir plywood sheathing
　　Two layers bitumen paper
　　Cedar shingles
4　Thermo glass rebated into 250- by 300-
　　millimeter fir posts
　　Glass held in place by vinyl zip strips
5　Concrete foundation pinned to natural
　　granite
　　100-millimeter granite facing

6

7

8

9

10

5   Section detail by Matt McLeod
6   East elevation on a winter night
7   Heavy timber frame of roof and
    window-wall
    Photography: Bo Heliwell
8   Living and dining room
    Photography: Greg Eymundson/Insight
9&10 Curve of roof after snowfall
    Photography: Leanna Rathkelly

granite base. Large sheets of thermo glass are directly set into the 10- by 12-inch (about 25.4- by 30.5-centimeter) fir timber posts to form the robust, simple window-wall frame.

The main bedroom is perched above the trees to take full advantage of the view. Its window bay and deck are supported on one massive log post like a giant birdhouse in the forest. The upper floor overlooks the gently sloping landscaped roof of the main floor level. This roof is the only cultivated landscape in the otherwise natural site. The combined roof load of the snow load and the landscaped roof is 4409 pounds per 10.8 square feet (2000 kilograms per square meter).

11 Alpine grass roof from stairwell
   Photography: Patrizia Menton
12 Library detail
   Photography:
   Greg Eymundson/Insight
13 Timber frame and stair
   Photography: John Fulker
14 Library window bay
   Photography: Patrizia Menton

11

12

13

14

I   Entry view
     Photography: Lyndal Williams
Opposite   East elevation (under construction)
     Photography: David O. Marlow

This 7000-square-foot (650.3-square-meter) residence has been designed for a 42-member family as a shared holiday retreat. The project is sited on the side of Aspen Mountain adjacent to the main ski slope (Little Nell) and the gondola.

The steep slope of the site meant that the steel and wood structure required extensive shoring, using 25-foot (7.6-meter) micropiles and soil nails. An inclinometer was installed upslope to monitor any movement in the site during construction. The site's steep incline also dictated the roof form with a maximum height limit at any point of 28 feet (8.5 meters) from existing or revised grade.

Due to the low pitch of the roofs, a zinc metal roof was chosen. Problems of dew points, which commonly occur within building envelopes with super-insulated roofs, meant the roof was designed to be a cold roof, with a 5.5-inch (140-millimeter) cold vented roof space above R38 insulation batts within the roof space below.

continued

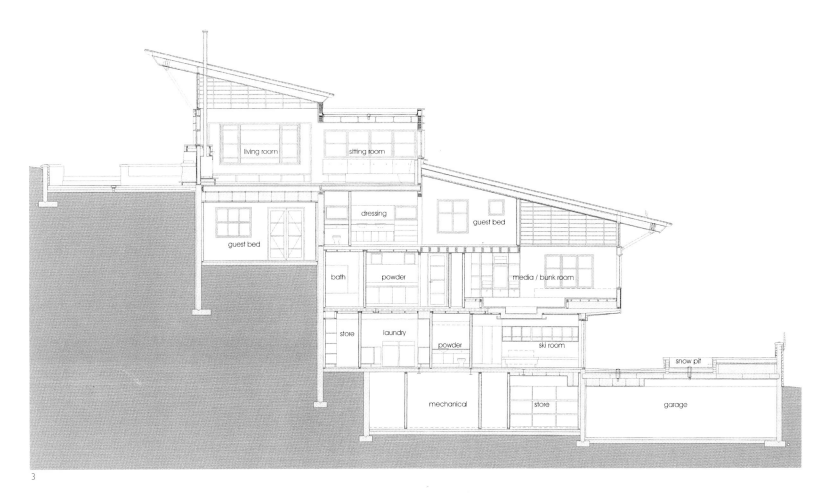

living room

sitting room

dressing

guest bed

guest bed

bath

powder

media / bunk room

store

laundry

powder

ski room

snow pit

mechanical

store

garage

3

Winter temperatures in Aspen can drop to around -10°F (-23°C) with an average annual snowfall of 180 inches (4.6 meters). Therefore, snow guards were designed to hold snow on each roof and the roofs were designed to shed onto non-trafficable areas—the landscaped area to the north of the dining room balcony, and to a drained flat membrane roof above the sitting area. On the house's north side, a rock-landscaped 'snow-pit,' which is removed from pedestrian traffic, catches the snow from the roof above, melts it and drains it away.

To capture the winter sun and views toward the mountain, clerestory windows are located on the south-facing walls. For views of the ski slope, windows have been added along the ski slope side of the house, while still maintaining a degree of privacy. A Low-E Sun 145

glass was chosen with a shading coefficient of 0.38, a UV block of 85 percent and overall U-value of 0.33 (R 3.0).

There were other challenges faced when designing this project for extreme weather conditions. Due to much of the house being below grade (because of the site's steep incline) a hot applied rubberized asphalt membrane was provided to all foundation walls to resist the hydrostatic pressure to which the foundation walls are exposed.

In addition, a complete underslab drainage system provides sub-surface drainage beneath the building due to concerns of local perched groundwater developing during times of heavy precipitation or seasonal runoff.

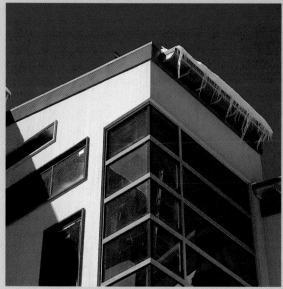

3 Cross section
4 Cold roof detail
5 Roof detail
6 Stair well
7 Entry canopy detail

Photography: David O. Marlow

8

9

10

garage

entry stair

store

electrical

lobby

mechanical

elev.

11

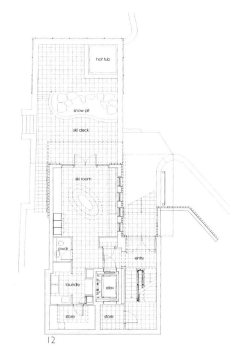

hot tub

snow pit

ski deck

ski room

pwdr

entry

laundry

elev.

store

store

12

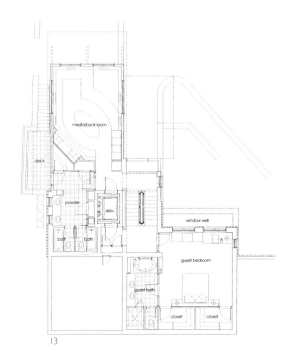

media/bunk room

deck

powder

elev.

window well

bath

bath

guest bedroom

guest bath

closet

closet

13

14

15

8   West elevation

9   Façade detail

10 Entry canopy

11 First floor plan

12 Second floor plan

13 Third floor plan

14 South courtyard

    Photography: David O. Marlow

15 Roof detail

    Photography: Lyndal Williams

National Museum of Wildlife Art

FENTRESS BRADBURN ARCHITECTS ■ Jackson Hole, Wyoming, USA

1

1　Entryway at night with Snow King resort ski area in background
2　Museum with Gros Ventre Butte in background
Photography: Timothy Hursley

Situated close to both the Grand Tetons and Yellowstone National Park, it was important for this museum to remain unobtrusive and to blend with the landscape. The building is located on a 70-acre site reclaimed from a scarred hillside—the result of previous insensitive commercial development. The museum twists with the site's topography, pivoting at a gulch that creases the hill, while stone cladding ensures that it blends with the site's natural features to resemble part of the rock outcropping.

Inside the museum, visitors enter down a stone stairway into a canyon-like lobby, with views of the surrounding mountains and valley. The galleries are secluded in the interior portion of the hillside, the design of which assists with balancing light and humidity exposure to the museum's art collection.

Throughout the year, Jackson Hole experiences considerable climate extremes. During summer, temperatures occasionally rise to around 86°F (30°C) while dropping to about

continued

2

3

4

5

5°F (-15°C) in winter. This meant that a number of cold climate design considerations were factored into the museum's overall design. For example, the building is oriented north to south to maximize on the sun warming the building throughout the morning, when the sun is low in the sky.

Heat loss is reduced in the building by super-insulated, double-wythe masonry, which also provides an important thermal barrier necessary for this hostile climate. In addition, earth-bermed construction shelters the museum's exhibit spaces, again helping to reduce heat loss.

Because environmental stability is vital for the preservation of fine art, glazing is limited to important interior spaces. This design minimizes thermal exposure to areas such as the exhibit hall where there is no glazing. When glass is used, predominantly in the lobby and administrative areas, it is with insulated glass units that provide efficient glass surfaces. All

7

8

glazing systems are also thermally broken to preclude conductive transfer. This is particularly important for controlling condensation because the museum's design maintains 45 percent relative humidity year round.

For the roof, an inverted membrane roofing system is designed so that the roof membrane acts as a vapor barrier. This is achieved by positioning the membrane on the warm side of the structure's insulation, which protects the membrane and controls condensation.

3   Entryway to museum from upper level parking
4   Windows to members' lounge
5   Rotunda connecting interior lobby to patio
Inset   Patio overlooking a national elk refuge
Photography: Timothy Hursley
7   Detail of stone-clad exterior wall
Photography: Nick Merrick/Hedrich-Blessing
8   Natural systems

10

11

Opposite Entry lobby from staircase leading
         to main floor
    10   Galleries display some of America's
         finest wildlife artists' work
    11   Fireplace detail demarcates entry
         to galleries
         Photography: Timothy Hursley

l   View of terrace facing the old mountain house

Opposite   West view of mountain

Photography: courtesy Aebi & Vincent Architects SIA AG

Recently, the Niesen Mountain House underwent renovation and extension work to modernize its image. Situated on a remote site 7664 feet (2336 meters) above sea level meant that special construction and technical installation requirements were necessary for the building. Steel was chosen as the primary structural material for the building's platform. This reduced the weight of parts to be assembled and therefore the cost of transportation. The heavier steel elements were transported and positioned on the mountain by helicopter, while remaining materials were transported along the Niesenbahn railway.

Given the exposed nature of the site, the platform is designed to withstand wind velocities of up to 167.8mph (270kph). The site's bedrock was also in poor condition so the structure was anchored on piles and driven into gravel. Larch wood flooring covers the total surface area of 9149 square feet (850 square meters) and was specially developed

continued

4

3

to meet the demands of the site. Similarly, the roof and gutters were constructed to resist high wind speeds and to prevent roof suction along its perimeter. The roof is made from prefabricated wood trusses covered with an aluminum-standing seam roof.

Sensitive renovation has taken place so that the façade of the old mountain house has been restored to its original appearance. The building was re-insulated and its interior was sympathetically redesigned. The new pavilion façade is a lightweight glass construction (reinforced with aluminum profiles) to maximize the alpine views.

In a location where temperatures can fall to -22°F (-30°C), heating was a key consideration. The site's extreme position made most alternative energy sources impractical. Therefore, oil

is stored in a frost-resistant tank and the oil supply pipe is heated to ensure it is always available to the building, even when experiencing the lowest temperatures. Radiators are situated along the glass façade of the restaurant while ventilation also supports heating with warm recycled air. In summer, when temperatures are significantly warmer (up to 68°F or 20°C), the building can be cooled without air-conditioning.

Additional installation requirements included pumping water from 2297 feet (700 meters) below up to the peak before it could be used for plumbing or drinking water. Sewage waste is collected in a sanitary building outside the house and then piped along the railway to the valley. The pipes and sanitary container are also heated to prevent freezing.

3 Night view
4 West view with backdrop of the
  alps (Eiger, Mönch and Jungfrau)
  Photography: Marcus Gyger
5 Northern view to mist-covered
  valley
6 Site plan
7 West terrace
  Photography: courtesy Aebi & Vincent
  Architects SIA AG

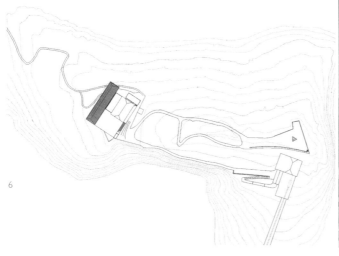

6

7

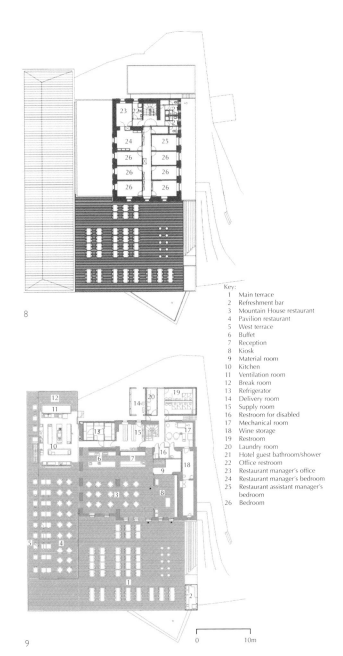

8

9

Key:
1   Main terrace
2   Refreshment bar
3   Mountain House restaurant
4   Pavilion restaurant
5   West terrace
6   Buffet
7   Reception
8   Kiosk
9   Material room
10 Kitchen
11 Ventilation room
12 Break room
13 Refrigerator
14 Delivery room
15 Supply room
16 Restroom for disabled
17 Mechanical room
18 Wine storage
19 Restroom
20 Laundry room
21 Hotel guest bathroom/shower
22 Office restroom
23 Restaurant manager's office
24 Restaurant manager's bedroom
25 Restaurant assistant manager's
    bedroom
26 Bedroom

0   10m

10

11

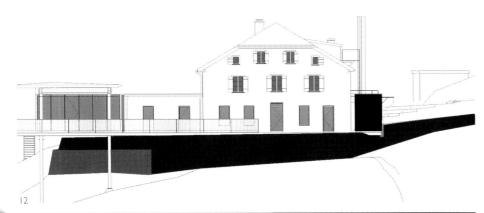

12

8 Second floor plan

9 First floor plan

10 Construction site during winter
   Photography: courtesy Aebi & Vincent Architects SIA AG

11 Detail: lightweight glass construction
   Photography: Adrian Scheidegger

12 South façade

13 Pavilion interior with view to alps

14 North façade

15 East façade

16 West façade
   Photography: courtesy Aebi & Vincent Architects SIA AG

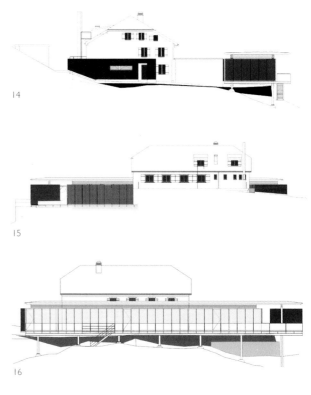

14

15

16

13

1   Terrace and hotel jut out over North Sea
2   Low-level resort blends into surrounding landscape
3   Restaurant with 180° sea views

The Nötsäter Conference & Sea Resort is planned for construction far out on the cliffs of Skärhamn, the main town on the island of Tjörn. As the sixth largest island of Sweden's west-coast archipelago, the fishing and freight trades have contributed to shaping Tjörn's community. The island is also a popular residential area and tourist destination, offering cultural and outdoor activities throughout summer and a bracing maritime climate during winter. Special care is taken to preserve the island's environmental and cultural inheritance.

Situated about 49.2 feet (15 meters) above sea level, the conference and holiday resort is 90,420 square feet (8400 square meters) and consists of a conference facility, a restaurant and 70 hotel rooms. A large roof spans most of the area and is covered with vegetation to minimize the building's impact on its natural surroundings. Under the roof is a weather-protected square entrance which has a dramatic view of the seascape beyond.

2

3

Once inside the building, visitors experience a double-height entrance hall with the North Sea as its backdrop, and conference rooms and the reception area positioned on either side. The double height of the ceiling continues out into a long, narrow restaurant and toward a large terrace located over the cliffs.

The rest of the building juts out over the water, supported by a major foundation column. This part of the building holds three floors of hotel rooms carried by 29.5-foot-high (9-meter-high) structural frameworks. The hotel comprises 36 suites and 35 double rooms, all with balconies and sea views. The balconies and the hotel structure's underside are clad in treated copper to weather harsh maritime and winter conditions.

Wingårdh Arkitektkontor's Nötsäter Conference & Sea Resort proposal is one of limited competition entries to locate a holiday and conference center in Skärhamn. At the time of publication the commission for this project was still to be decided.

1

2

Designed and constructed in the midst of the early 1980s oil crisis, this landmark structure continues to maintain its place as one of the most energy-efficient commercial buildings in the world. Located in view of Niagara Falls, where wind chill in December through February hovers a few degrees below freezing, and in summer temperatures can reach around 77°F (25°C), the Occidental Chemical Center is one of the original 'intelligent buildings.'

The design represents a unique 'double-skin' approach, using a building envelope that is changeable, dynamic, and able to respond to the climatic environment, much the same as some living creatures have evolved to adjust their skins automatically to different conditions of heat and cold. The concept was to create a 'living' building able to adapt to its environment, even as that environment may change from day to night and season to season.

1 Building is sited on the axis of Rainbow Bridge from Canada, with a view of Niagara River and Gorge to south, west and north

2 Night view reveals louvers and inner glazed wall

3 Temperature-achieved sensors control vents in space between two glass skins to admit heat into offices

4 Painted aluminum louvers are 'off-the-shelf' units often used as dampers for high-velocity applications

5 Void between outer and inner walls allows heat build-up in sunny conditions, which can be vented at the roof

Photography: Patricia Layman Bazelon

The building's exterior consists of two glass walls, 4 feet (about 1.2 meters) apart between which is an automatically operated louver system adapted from 'off-the-shelf' components. During the occupied daytime period, the louvers track the sun to provide virtually complete solar shielding of the building interior. During unoccupied periods, the louvers close to create a fully insulated shell. The passive solar potential derived from daylighting is maximized as the exterior skin is glass from floor to ceiling, and the louvers provide much-needed light diffusion at all times. Through the automatically controlled damper operation of vented space between the glass skins, solar heat is either collected (trapped) or rejected (purged) depending on building demand.

When constructed, the building was believed to be the largest passive solar collector in the world and the most energy-efficient structure of its kind.

The 236,000-square-foot (22,000-square-meter) Hamar Olympic Hall was the arena for speed skating during the 1994 Winter Olympics. The hall is located in the flat wetlands of Åkersvika, surrounding the town of Hamer (north of Oslo). Here, structures are exposed to all types of weather, from mild summers to freezing winters.

The concept for the building's distinctive design is the 'Viking ship.' Norway has had a longstanding tradition of boat construction and, in shape and form, the hall's roof closely resembles the lower hull of the old and beautiful Oselver boats.

The huge roof structure is given the necessary lightness and flexibility through this design theme, liberating it from the static shape of the arena itself. However, this construction has an extremely complex geometry. For example, the laminated wood support arches have 10 different length spans and 10 different roof heights.

The roof also needed to be heavily insulated to conserve heat in the hall's interior and to prevent it escaping through such a large and exposed roof surface. The vast structure comprises layers of felt, mineral wool, insulation, a vapor barrier and steel sheeting.

3

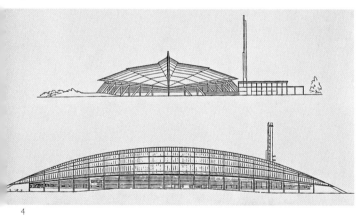

4

5

6

1   Building resembles a giant
     upturned boat
Inset Timber structure exposed
     during construction
3   Wide-angled interior view
4   Longitudinal section and
     cross section
5   Construction details in
     timber roof structure
6   Roof structure rests on
     exterior concrete supports
Photography: Jiri Havran

To maximize on short winter daylight hours, it was important to admit light into the hall's interior through the use of polycarbonate, which is more economical than glass for such an expansive surface. This also brings the roof's laminated arches to life and describes the play of lines along the length of the roof against the horizontal beams.

As the building will always be seen against the blue horizon it was decided to give the large roof a subtle blue-gray colour. Only one accentuating colour was used—a fresh, joyful green, symbolizing sport, outdoor activity, and happiness—which is featured on some exterior surfaces and on the hall's interior.

All details were simplified as much as possible to make the building durable. Oiled iron doors were used to protect against the elements and a mesh snow catcher on the roof prevents dangerous snow shed.

The original log structure for this residence was built in the mid-1970s with little regard for building codes. As with many older log structures, settlement and twisting had occurred, leaving rooms with sloping floors and irregular-shaped walls. This was partly due to the use of green logs in construction and a result of Jackson Hole's climate extremes. Temperatures can fall to around -20°F (-28.9°C) in winter with extremes of -46°F (-43.3°C) and soar to the high 90°F (the high 30°C) in summer.

The alternate freeze-thaw action caused by temperature extremes can wreak havoc with poor or improperly prepared foundations. Part of the project's new design needed to address this problem. The decision was made to physically raise all the floors, level their underpinnings and then lower them back down. The existing roof was also restructured and reinforced to ensure building code conformity.

1 Snow-covered
   house at night
2 North elevation
3 East elevation
4 West elevation

The new owner's directive was to completely remodel the existing house and to integrate a 2000-square-foot (185.8-square-meter) addition that included a two-car garage with two guest suites above. As well as emphasizing the existing home's rustic charms, the building had to be modernized to comply with current building standards, and the owners wanted to improve its functional organization. For example, better circulation between spaces,

more effective use of storage opportunities in undereave areas, and comfortable living and entertaining rooms became the main criteria for the remodeling effort.

Existing log walls were all refinished to a smooth texture. Flat quartzite stone was introduced to places such as the hearth and chimney chase, entryway, and kitchen, as a counterpoint to the smooth wood and plaster surfaces. The kitchen was reconfigured for

continued

5

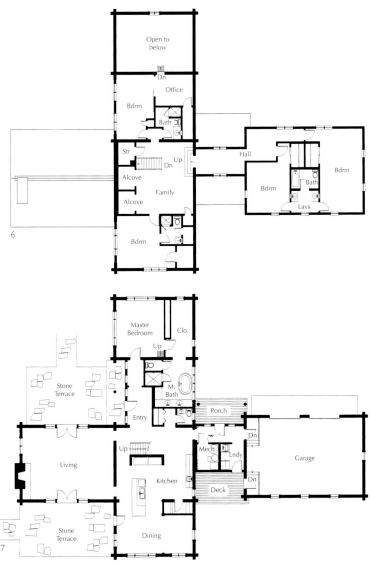

6

7

functionality and equipped with a full complement of professional-grade appliances, stainless-steel counters, and preparation and serving areas.

In the bedrooms, sleeping alcoves and storage closets were built into low ceiling spaces where the roof meets the sidewalls. Old, inefficient baseboard heaters were replaced with a hydronic radiant heating system that serves the entire house. A second hydronic system keeps walkways and terraces free of ice and snow for safe passage and outdoor entertaining during the winter holidays.

9

5   Remodeled house retains
    its original rustic charm
6   Second floor plan
7   First floor plan
8   Living room with quartzite
    hearth and chimney chase
9   Cosy sleeping alcoves in
    family room
10 Reconfigured kitchen with
    stainless-steel appliances
Photography: Cameron Neilson

10

Rafferty House

ALFREDO DE VIDO ■ Stratton, Vermont, USA

This privately owned residence is situated on a steep site with views toward distant mountains. Due to this location, the house was planned on three levels, each with generous window areas to maximize the views.

The entrance to the home is at the top level; the living room, master bedroom and other main spaces take up the middle level; and the lower level contains bunks, a game room, and a sauna.

During summer, Vermont generally experiences daytime temperatures in the mid-70°F (low-20°C) while throughout winter they drop to around the low-20°F (a few degrees Centigrade below freezing). The mean winter snowfall varies depending on elevation but can be anything from around 100 inches (2.5 meters) to over 250 inches (6.4 meters).

For effective snow removal from the home's entrance during winter, a wood bridge rises above the ground of the sloped site to meet the entrance door.

3

4

1 View from south at dusk
2 North entrance with bridge
3 West façade
4 Living room with masonry
   fireplace
Inset Glazed bedroom admits
     sunlight from south
Photography: Bill Maris

In addition to the substantially glazed areas designed for views, rows of skylights on the building's south side complement these windows to ensure as much winter solar gain as possible. Windows have also been placed strategically throughout this home to lessen heat loss during colder months. For example, there are few glazed openings to the east, west, and north sides of the house for this reason.

To conserve heat in this wood-framed house, insulation has been added to its roofs, slabs, and opaque walls. The predominantly glazed south-facing walls are also constructed from absorptive masonry surfaces on their interior to store the sun's warmth.

Stratified air in the main south-facing room is recirculated to level temperatures within.

The Red House is located in the western suburbs of Oslo on the east bank of a heavily wooded river valley. Despite the site's suburban context, surrounding fir and pine trees offer seclusion and provide the illusion that the building lies somewhere far more remote. The house is positioned perpendicular to the river to heighten the setting's dramatic potential and to avoid obstructing views from the home.

The project is organized on two floors. Living spaces and the parents' bedroom are located on the top (entry) floor, oriented south and toward the views beyond. A covered terrace among the trees to the west extends this level. Downstairs, on the lower level, are the children's bedrooms and a family room, facing the valley to the north. This double orientation is the basis for the project's architectonic dymanic, and in all the house's dimensions design focuses on enhancing this theme.

1   View from river valley
2   South façade
3   Entrance
4   Bedroom window facing
    valley to north

2

3

4

In a country which experiences freezing temperatures and short daylight hours during winter, lighting was an important factor in this home's design. Trees surround the building's north and west façades so extensive fenestration wraps much of the house in order to maximize natural lighting to its interior. For example, on the lower level, strip windows facing north and west invite daylight into the darker side of the house. Upstairs, further strip windows and wall-to-ceiling glass sliding doors to the terrace allow for ample daylighting at this level.

Perhaps most striking in the site's winter surroundings, is the vibrant red colour of the building's stained wood exterior. In stark contrast to its frosty setting, the house shines out reflecting, says the architect, its owner's temperament and the name of the suburb in which it is located (Røa, meaning red).

123

5

5   Living room window
     facing south
6   South façade detail
7   North façade detail
8&9 Terrace
10,11&12 Main floor

6

7

8

9

10

11

12

125

13

14

15

13　View toward entrance

14　Kitchen

15　Sliding door opens living
　　room to terrace

16&17　Living room

18　Basement corridor with
　　workspace

Photography: Nils Petter Dale

16

17

18

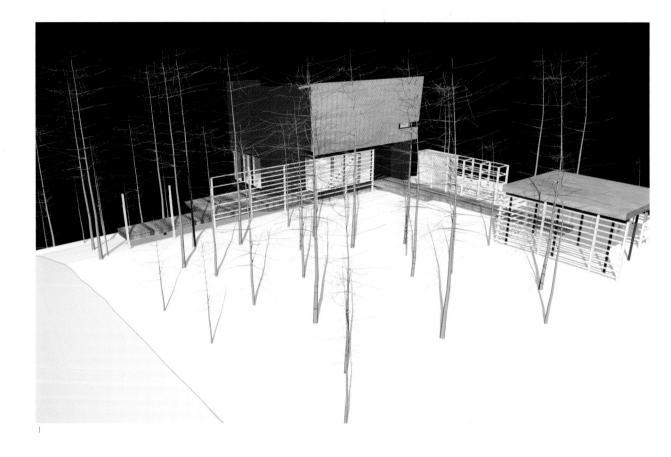

The site for this house, which was under construction at the time of publication, is a tree-lined hillside overlooking the vast St Lawrence River in Kamouraska, Quebec. Typical winter weather conditions in this region of Quebec can be severe with sub-zero temperatures and considerable snowfall.

Given the small budget for this project (US$41,000), the design does not make any grand architectural gestures. Instead it focuses on more fundamental elements such

as the realization of the building envelope, including insulation, damp protection, and thermal-glazed windows.

The house is constructed from wood and steel and the project is defined by a simple wood volume. A steel ventilated roof spreads over this volume in a protective manner. The ventilated roof design was chosen to reduce heat loss in winter and heat gain in summer.

3

4

1 Bird's-eye view of house, garage,
   footbridge, storage and terrace
2 Entrance to house via footbridge
3 View from southeast with terrace
   extension
4 Wood screen detail provides
   privacy and shelter
5 North elevation facing the
   St Lawrence River

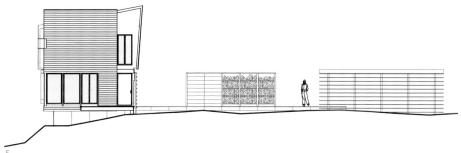

5

The approach to the house from the undercover garage is via a wooden 'footbridge,' raised from the ground. In winter, this 'footbridge' will allow easy snow removal and access to the house over the snow-covered ground. A second 'footbridge/terrace' runs to the left of the house and is framed by a wood screen. During the summer the screen acts as an effective shading device but in winter it will allow plenty of light to penetrate the home's interior from the south.

Inside the house, the interior structure is exposed to illustrate the construction principle for this building. Circulation is designed to create transition zones between external spaces and interior spaces and between each of the house's three levels. A fireplace in the living room provides heat to the first and second floors of the house through vents in the second floor.

A natural integration of architecture with the land was important for this project, in order to minimize its impact on the environment. Therefore, little landscaping will be done to the surrounding area, only a new planting zone directly in front of the residence.

This 30,000-square-foot (2787-square-meter) complex is located by Lake Inari in northern Lapland, which is situated some 150 miles (241.4 kilometers) north of the Arctic Circle. The project involved the construction of the Sámi Lapp Museum next to the existing outdoor museum into a joint facility that now also includes the Northern Lapland Visitor Center. The Sámi Lapp Museum continues to document the cultural heritage of the Sámi culture, which still thrives today. The Northern Lapland

Visitor Center provides an educational resource and services for nature lovers and visitors to the area.

The two facilities are housed in four volumes clad in variously stained pine. These buildings are at once reminiscent of Lapland's traditional rural architecture while remaining distinctly modern. Design was also influenced by the need to ensure

2

4

3

1   View from open-air museum
    Photography: Jussi Tiainen

2   Indoor ramp leading to exhibition floor,
    outdoor ramp leading to open-air museum

3&4   View from parking area toward main entrance
    Photography: Rauno Träskelin

minimal impact to the buildings' surrounding natural environment and consideration of the area's dramatic climatic changes.

In this region, winter temperatures drop to as much as -58°F (-50°C) and rarely rise above (59°F) 15°C in summer. Areas north of the Arctic Circle also experience 'polar days' or 'white nights' during summer, when the sun never sets. In winter, 'polar nights' set in for about two months when the sun does not rise above the horizon.

Within the complex, multiple sources of artificial and natural light have been installed to counter the extremes of light experienced year-round. Uplighting warms the interior's curved ceilings, while hanging lights and spotlighting detail exhibition displays and designated areas throughout the complex. Extensive glazing and skylighting also admit natural light to the buildings' interiors.

5&6   Main entrance
      Photography: Rauno Träskelin
   7 Main entrance
      Photography: Jussi Tiainen
   8 South end of museum and ramp leading to exhibition floor
   9 Second-floor lobby
  10 Introductory exhibition on natural and cultural time scales
11&12 Permanent exhibition of Lapland and Sámi culture
      Photography: Rauno Träskelin

9

10

11

12

1

Sanga-Säby Courses & Conferences complex is located 21.75 miles (35 kilometers) northwest of Stockholm on an island in Lake Mälaren. The complex is an example of traditional business interests being successfully combined with a high level of environmental responsibility.

Due to the complex's location—an area of natural beauty and a valuable water source—environmental considerations were paramount when deciding on the architectural design,

1 View to sauna, relaxation area and pool at waterfront

2 Building façade follows contour of hill

134

continued

3

4

building materials, construction methods, inventories, and furnishings for the project. A number of energy-efficient and conservation methods were implemented as a result. For example, the complex's heating—an important consideration for an area which hits sub-zero temperatures in winter—is entirely non-fossil-fuel based, relying on heat pumps and solar heating instead.

The latest addition to the project is the new Mälarblick hotel building, housing 16 guestrooms on a south-facing plateau overlooking the lake. Again, design and construction followed strict environmental safeguards. The intention was to provide first-class accommodation with as little negative environmental impact as possible.

The building is constructed from wood, of which 70 percent is FSC-certified (taken from certified well-managed forests). The hotel was designed to fit into its surroundings causing minimal disturbance to natural vegetation and materials during construction.

To combat the cold winters, a water-based floor heating system has been installed in this building too. This system is heated through solar collectors located on the roof. Quadruple-glazed windows and a roof cover of natural sedum assist with insulation. Sunshades, which are set almost horizontally, protect against low-lying winter sun and provide welcome shade during warmer summer months.

3　Large windows maximize outside views
4　Sunshades are designed to admit winter sun into interior
5　Indoor pool is located at the same level as lake's surface
6　Laminated glass is the only division between pool and lake

Photography: Åke E:son Lindman

5

6

The site for this project is located on a steep, north-facing slope within an alpine ski village at the base of a mountain. Temperatures in Thredbo drop to around 21.2°F (-6°C) in winter and reach around 69.8°F (21°C) during summer.

Sastrugi Lodge is a repaired and refurbished 1959 Heritage-listed building with pavilion additions reflecting the curved plan and pitch of the original structure. The new pavilions are set back from the original in a counter curve to define the original

building form. They are also set into the hill, minimizing their apparent scale next to the original, while doubling the available floor space. Different materials define the new work from the old. The mono pitch roof is constructed from zinc sheet with timber, stone, and metal façades.

The additions, through the continued use of this geometry, reinforce the original plan but also provide the optimum engineering solution for a site subject to landslides.

1 Lodge in snow
2 Western cover of original
   house with new ski room
3 Lodge's zinc roof looking west

They were built after the tragic Thredbo landslides of 1999, caused by melting snow, which destabilized very steep north-facing slopes heavily built up with lightweight 50s structures. As a result, this project anchors the original structure to the hill geometrically by transferring the downhill forces away from the building; much like a dam transfers loads to the side of the curved spillway.

The building's setting into the ground and across the contours also responds to the best possible solar orientation, which works well to insulate the structure. In addition, the building's internal ambient temperature is comfortably maintained without central heating by two open fireplaces, underfloor slab heating and double-glazing. The lodge was also painted black to maximize its response to the cold climate of the surrounding Snowy Mountains.

4

5

6

7

8

10

9

4   North elevation in snow
5   Original portion of northern
    elevation and new deck
6   New northern deck
7   Living area at night
8   Stone fireplace
9   View from kitchen area
    to dining beyond
10 Ski storage with car
    spaces above

Photography: Robert Brown

Sibelius Hall

ARTTO PALO ROSSI TIKKA ARCHITECTS ■ Lahti, Finland

This project provides a flexible space which includes a concert hall and congress venue. The building is located on the site of an old timber furniture factory in Ankkuri, the former industrial heart of Lahti, which has recently undergone considerable rejuventation. The new hall connects to the original factory, which is protected as a significant cultural and historical building, although sympathetic renovation was required due to the factory's derelict condition.

The 78,150-square-foot (7260-square-meter) project includes the concert and congress hall which seats 1100 people, a public lobby, artists' spaces, rehearsal and conference rooms, and 6458 square feet (600 square meters) of exhibition space. The complex enjoys a panoramic view of Lake Vesijärvi.

Wood provides an important design theme for this building. It relates not only to the factory's historical purpose but also to the lake, which, for years, has been a vital

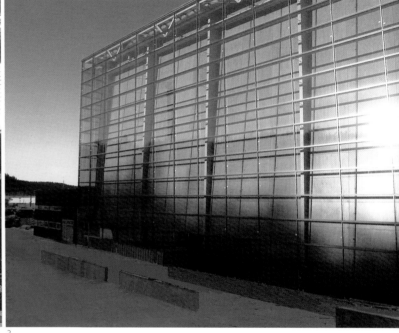

2   3

means of transporting timber to the nearby railway. Wood is used as the predominant building material throughout the project, for example to provide warm inviting interiors for winter concert goers. It also influences the design of spaces like the Forest Hall—a tall one-story space which connects the old factory with the new hall. Huge wooden girders support the structure and their design is reminiscent of a Finnish forest.

In an area where winter temperatures may plummet to -40°F (-40°C) but reach 104°F (40°C) in summer, coping with extreme temperatures is an important design consideration. For instance, in this region, external wall structures are generally heavy to provide added insulation. However, a problem for this project was that wood is a relatively light material.

continued

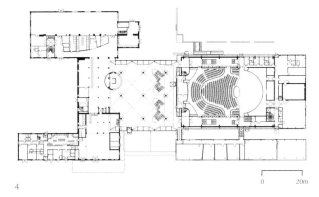

4

5

6

7

0   20m

In the shoe-box-shaped Sibelius Hall, an additional priority was to provide suitable soundproofing while maintaining excellent acoustics within the hall. A solid acoustical wooden wall was required to absorb outside noise and reflect sound back into the concert hall. This is part of a multi-layered façade cased in a glass skin which is supported by horizontal beams to further diminish outside noise. Free air space between the glass skin and acoustical wall are essential for both the hall's sound and for providing insulation to the building's interior.

The complex's extensive glazing also attracts light into its interior even on the shortest days, and is double-glazed to prevent heat loss.

Sibelius Hall

8

9

10

11

4   Floor plan
5   Reverberation chamber
6   Concert hall, first balcony
    Photography: Voitto Niemelä
7   Openable plywood
    'doors' in concert hall, to
    adjust the acoustics
    Photography: Mikko Auerniitty
8   Longitudinal section:
    rendering by Tomas
    Westerholm, Render Oy
9   View from technical
    balcony
10 View from choir gallery
11 Gallery structures
    in concert hall
    Photography: Voitto Niemelä

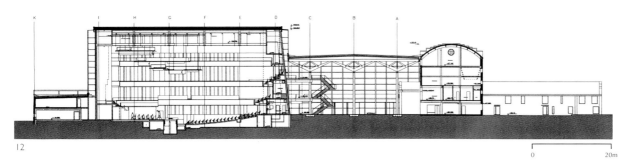

12

12 Section

13 Forest Hall, congress wing, and
   concert hall from Lake Versijärvi
   Photography: Mikko Auerniitty

14 Main entrance
   Photography: Voitto Niemelä

15 Sibelius Hall in winter
   Photography: Mikko Auerniitty

16 Wooden structures of
   Forest Hall

17 Night rendering by Tomas
   Westerholm, Render Oy

18 Furnishings in Forest Hall
   Photography: Voitto Niemelä

13

14

15

16

17

18

This house is situated close to the ski lifts and slopes of Ramundberget ski resort in central Sweden. The aim was to create a modern home, which takes full advantage of the surrounding views while, maintaining a certain amount of privacy from the nearby slopes and ski lifts.

In order to comply with local building authorities, it was also important that the building should be in keeping with the traditional architecture in the area. For example, the

building's façade is constructed from horizontal pinewood paneling. Its light gray shade was achieved through a simple process using Ferro sulphate to 'weather' the home so that it would fit in with the older houses in the area. By contrast, the oiled wooden surfaces of the window- and doorframes offer a hint of the house's light wood interior.

The front porch, which is traditionally adorned with decorative Baroque ornaments, has been simplified and modernized. During the warmer summer months, it serves as

1   Lodge is located next to a ski run
    Photography: Bruno Ehrs
2   Numerous windows admit natural
    light to interior
    Photography: Hans Murman

a south-facing patio. The house also has a peat roof, typical of the area. This is a well-functioning material both in summer and winter, when it 'collects' snow to provide a natural insulating layer.

Inside, the use of pine dominates, again this is a traditional material, used for this building type. The design is simple. The interior is basically one large room with a 'box' in it, which contains the bedroom

continued

2

3

and bathroom. A number of incisions have been made into this area to permit as much winter sunlight as possible.

The roof and walls of the house are both insulated, while under-floor heating and ceiling heat panels provide warmth to the interior. Apart from two large windows offering mountain views, windows have been kept small and to a minimum, to cut down on energy consumption.

In an area where winter sports are so prominent, the house would not be complete without a sauna. This is located on the lower mezzanine floor with pinewood benches and walls dressed in birch bark.

4

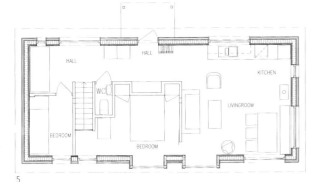

5

6

3 Exterior view with valley beyond

    Photography: Bruno Ehrs

4 Modern windows offer views onto surrounding landscape

5 Ground floor

6 Mezzanine floor

7 The winter landscape is enjoyed both inside and out

    Photography: Hans Murman

7

8

11

8   Living area with wood-
     burning stove
     Photography: Bruno Ehrs

Inset   Kitchen and living area
         featuring bedroom 'box'
         Photography: Hans Murman

10   Master bedroom
     Photography: Bruno Ehrs

11   Birch bark detail of
     sauna walls
     Photography: Hans Murman

10

This is a two-level, 430,600-square-foot (40,000-square-meter) enclosed shopping mall in a rapidly expanding suburb of Reykjavik. It is anchored by major stores at each end and encloses a public square with restaurants and cinemas.

Swept by the Gulf Stream and bordering the Arctic, Reykjavik has a generally cool/mild climate, frequently wet and windy with periods of intense sub-zero temperatures. Winters are gray and depressing, while summers have almost continuous daylight. Up to 180 freeze-thaw cycles with often-rapid temperature changes constantly challenge the Icelanders with ice, snow, and flooding. Winds can reach over 100mph (160.9kph).

The architectural responses to these climatic challenges have been both visual and technical. Unusually for a building with a roof area of 20,000 square feet (1858 square meters), the whole is enclosed within a sloping roof. All plant is internal, with

2

3

4

air intakes and extracts heated and drained to prevent snow and ice build-up. The continuous curving roof also prevents the build up of drifting snow.

In Iceland, the sun's high UV content normally fades all strong colors but the shopping center's façades are clad with deep-blue, stove-enameled steel panels that will not fade. To optimize light, the mall's continuous glazed roof is raised to catch even the lowest rays of winter sunshine, while internal solar shades reflect light into the interior. These shades also prevent excessive solar glare throughout summer and are floodlit on winter nights in order to create a friendly interior.

The building is heavily insulated and, as Reykjavik is supplied with geothermal water, there are no boilers. Where shops require air-conditioning, natural cold water is used for chilling. Hot water is piped under the surface of parking areas and footpaths. Parking areas are also kept free of obstructions to allow snow-clearing machines to operate.

5

6

7

0   50m

Although the building is over 656 feet (199.9 meters) long, there are no major expansion joints. This is partly due to the cold climate and the building being built halfway into the lava bedrock. The heavily insulated concrete structure is topped with an aluminum roof supported by a steel frame. Exposed entrances have revolving doors to combat the wind.

8

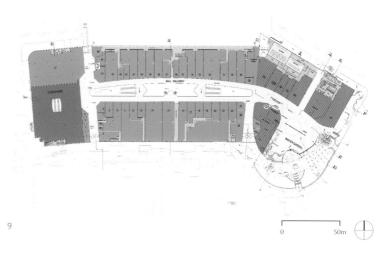

9

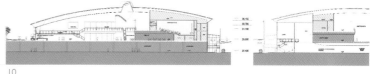

10

0   50m

5   Site plan
6   View from south
7   View from southwest
8   Mall at night
    Photography: David Barbour
9   Upper floor plan
10 Winter Garden section

11

12

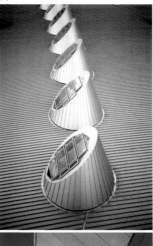

15

11   Mall under construction
12   Mall interior with Christmas
     decorations
     Photography:
     Helgi Mar Halldoresson
13   Mall interior
     Photography: David Barbour
14   Roof lights
15   Cladding detail
     Photography: Richard Allen

Completed in 2001, this cottage is conveniently located in Herlíkovice ski resort in the Krkonoše Mountains, just outside a protected area of national park. The cottage is situated right next to a ski run and opposite a ski lift, and provides an alpine retreat throughout winter and a welcome family getaway during summer.

The new structure occupies a site area of 538.2 square feet (50 square meters) on the foundations of an old derelict cottage. In keeping with the client's requirements and financial budget, it remains simple in design and minimal in size. The client wanted a residence that was basic but comfortable, which would not distract from the enjoyment and wellbeing of its surroundings.

From the outside, the cottage presents a simple shape, blind to the north and to the ski lift but enjoying views of the slope and forest to the south through large windows.

2

3

4

1 North view from ski lift
2 Northeast view from valley
3 View from northeast
   Photography: Ivan Kroupa
4 Southwest view from ski run
   Photography: Libor Jebavy
5 East view from forest
   Photography: Ivan Kroupa

This side of the cottage also features a protected terrace, which extends the whole structure and gives it its proportion within the local context.

The cottage's interior comprises a continuous two-story space with wood finishes. The building's circulation has been dictated by the need to include essential interior equipment in a small area. An additional feature is the comfortable bench seating wrapped around the walls on either side of the fireplace in the main living area.

5

6   Entrance to interior from terrace
    Photography: Ivan Kroupa
7   Terrace detail
    Photography: Libor Jebavy
8   West façade detail
9   Protected main entrance
10 Living area with kitchen and fireplace
11 Stairs to children's area in attic
12 Stairs with view to living area
13 Bench seating under stairs leading to
    master bedroom
    Photography: Ivan Kroupa

10

11

12   13

Snow King Inn
ALFREDO DE VIDO ■ Jackson Hole, Wyoming, USA

This 204-room hotel and conference center functions as both a ski resort and as a summer entrance to Yellowstone National Park. It is located at the edge of Jackson's residential area, at the base of Snow King Mountain.

Natural wood materials have been widely used for this project's construction, due to wood's long wearability and high rot resistance in this low-humidity, high-altitude area. In addition, considerable winter snowfall means that covered parking areas were a necessary design feature in order to provide snow-free arrival and departure for visitors.

The building's insulated, pitched roofs also prevent heavy snow accumulation, while directing snow shed onto designated areas below to avoid pedestrian accidents. Small balconies off the guestrooms are hung from the roof structure to avoid the supports penetrating the roofs' snowy cover and creating possible snow-clearing

continued

1 Front view of hotel with log cabins in foreground
2 Front of hotel with ski slopes in background
3 Rear of hotel
4 Roof structure uses local heavy timber construction

4

5

6

7

8

problems. These balconies are accessed from rooms through large glazed openings, which admit sun into individual rooms and open onto beautiful views.

Inside the hotel a central atrium space faces onto the surrounding ski slopes and opens all public areas to the sun, attracting as much daylight as possible to the building's interior. A huge stone fireplace focuses the space and provides a warm meeting space for guests in the heart of the hotel.

The building's heating system is electric with coils in slab areas and baseboards in individual rooms, due to the availability of inexpensive hydro-electric power from the nearby Columbia River system.

5 Interior view toward dining area
6 Interior of atrium
7 Atrium looking under bridge
8 Atrium looking toward fireplace
9 Lobby and entrance hall
10 View to ceiling showing room access via balconies

Photography: Louis Reens

9

10

The old Turtagrø Hotel, which has been the starting point for climbing in the Hurrungane Mountains for more than 100 years, burnt down in 2001. The mountain range is situated in Jotunheimen National Park, west Norway, some 222 miles (357.3 kilometers) north of Oslo.

With the new hotel, the owner wanted to recreate some of the old building's atmosphere—a recognizable scale, spatial sequence, colors, and materials. A nearby timber annex also remains from the original hotel. However, the new building required a different architectonic expression and an efficient layout.

All communal functions have been placed on the basement floor or the ground floor around a small reception, with all guestrooms on the first and second floors. It was a challenge to combine large capacity with the necessary intimacy in the communal areas. The guestrooms differ from conventional hotel rooms in that they have no

2   3   4

1   Hotel's entrance stairway is
    an important meeting place
2   Starting point for climbing,
    hiking, and skiing
3   Entrance
4   Old annex

ante-space and are shallower and wider than normal. This design ensures a more open connection between the bedroom and bathroom. The interiors are robust and simple.

The building's architectonic expression links it to the surrounding mountains, incorporating three ascending tower suites. The architecture sets up a dialogue with the landscape while stonewalls, carved panel surfaces, and recessed glazing relate to the existing annex.

The hotel has a steel structure and prefabricated decks, which span between external walls to give the building plan full freedom. Its exterior is clad with timber paneling, felt shingles, and stone. The interior features lime-washed paneling, painted wooden floors, and oiled oak.

continued

5

Despite its moderate altitude compared with other mountain range areas, Jotunheimen's northern latitude gives the area a typical high-alpine climate. Rapid weather changes are commonplace, even in summer, while winter can be bleak with snow, flooding rivers, and short days.

The hotel is well equipped to deal with such unpredictable conditions. Large windows allow as much daylighting as possible but, to avoid heat loss, double-glazing has been

installed with an insulating value of 1.4. The hotel walls are also wood-covered with 7.9-inch-thick (20-cm-thick) stonefiber insulation. Electric heating is used throughout the hotel with the added benefit of fireplaces located in communal areas.

The roof of the hotel is also lined with 11.8-inch-thick (30-cm-thick) insulation. Its wooden and steel structure has been designed to withstand snow loads of up to 110.2 stone (700kg) of snow per 10.8 square feet (1 square meter).

7

8

6

9

5   Hotel and old annex

6   View from hotel toward
    mountain peaks

7   Window provides outlook
    from reception

8&9 Hotel at night

10

11

12

13

14

10   Local stone is used for landscaping

11   Annex detail

12   Annex terrace

13   Dining

14   Communal area

Photography: Nils Petter Dale

Building in Jackson Hole can be difficult and not only because of its extreme climate and considerable snowfall. Temperatures range from around -20°F (-28.9°C) in winter with extremes of -46°F (-43.3°C) to the high 90°F (the high 30°C) in summer. The area has a mean annual snowfall of 150 inches (381 centimeters). Building codes also stipulate that structures must be designed to withstand the possibility of earthquakes with up to 4 feet (1.2 meters) of wet snow on their roofs.

This is because Jackson Hole, the gateway for tourists visiting Grand Teton and Yellowstone National Parks, is situated on a major slip fault.

Log cabins are good structures for enduring seismic events as they possess a tremendous ability to move without breaking apart or failing. The use of saddle notches in corners and properly placed shear pins enables a low-level log structure

continued

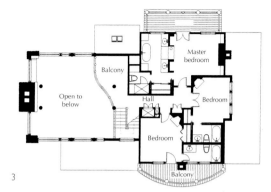

3

4

5

1   Bed and Breakfast was built to withstand four feet (1.2 meters) of wet snow

2   Guest cabin in which owner lived during renovation of original home

3   Second floor plan

4   First floor plan

5   Basement floor plan

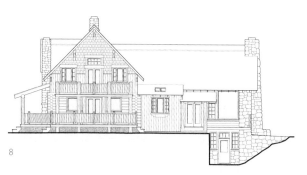

8

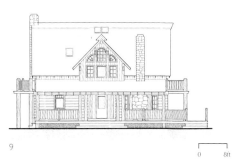

9

0   8ft

to successfully resist all but the most dramatic earthquakes without the use of stiff moment frames. However, older structures, which do not have the benefit of such engineering or construction, will show the effects of quake activity.

The original structure of the Twin Mountain Bed and Breakfast Lodge had floors that were 3 inches (7.6 centimeters) out of level, and gable end walls that were as much as 1 foot (30.5 centimeters) out of plumb. In order to adapt and re-use the structure, the interior walls were gutted and the structure stabilized. The walls were literally pulled back into plumb and the floors were jacked up and leveled.

Heavily loaded beams, such as those under high snow loads, tend to progressively fail in a seismic event, like tumbling dominoes. The points of connection between beams and columns are critical to resisting this tendency so structural engineers were consulted. With their guidance, a system of stiff support frames, each of which is capable of withstanding the combined effects of snow and quake, was installed. Covered porches were also added to keep snowfall and weather away from entrances, and to protect some of the log structure from the effects of sun. The transformation of an old log cabin into the warm, inviting, and safe retreat of the Twin Mountain Bed and Breakfast Lodge was complete.

l   External view with
     garage to left
Opposite   View from northwest
     in winter

This 1399-square-foot (130-square-meter) house is situated on the shores of a picturesque lake. The client's brief was simple—that the house should contain three bedrooms, a bathroom, a living room with kitchen area, and a garage for the car. The bedrooms, bathroom, and garage are designed in a perpendicular block facing the forest, while the shape of the living room follows the lake's shoreline. Large windows open to the lake, visually expanding the room and making the most of the views beyond.

This recreational home is ideally located to suit Lithuania's varied climate. In summer, when the temperature can reach over 86°F (30°C), people are drawn to the Baltic Sea or lakes for swimming or sunbathing. In winter, when the temperature may drop to around 13°F (-25°C), people still enjoy the snow, ice, and outdoor winter sports.

Given such weather conditions, careful consideration was required when choosing suitable building materials. Lithuanians traditionally like to use clay bricks and

continued

3

4

wood, which are local materials well suited to the climate. Wood logs are unique in combining excellent insulation qualities and natural breathability. Wood keeps in the heat on cold days but also lets in a suitable amount of air, ensuring proportional warmth and humidity inside the house.

Wood is also easy to maintain. Only a special façade varnish was used to preserve the villa's natural colour. Although this area can experience rigorous, wind, rain, and snow, these

elements only serve to naturally weather the building's external timber surface. Inside, using a 'warm' material like wood also means that minimal interior decoration was required.

In Lithuania, log houses are usually prepared and assembled at the construction company's main base. Then they are dismantled, moved to and reassembled in their chosen location. This means that construction can take place during the colder months of the year so that the project can then be realized during the warmer months.

3 View from northwest
4 View from southeast in winter
5 View from north
6 Exterior wood detail

5

6

7 Living area with view to lake

8 Living/dining area with large glazed windows

9 Exterior wood detail

10 Exterior wood detail and roof supports

11 Ground floor plan

Photography: Raimondas Urbakavičius

7

8

8182

9

10

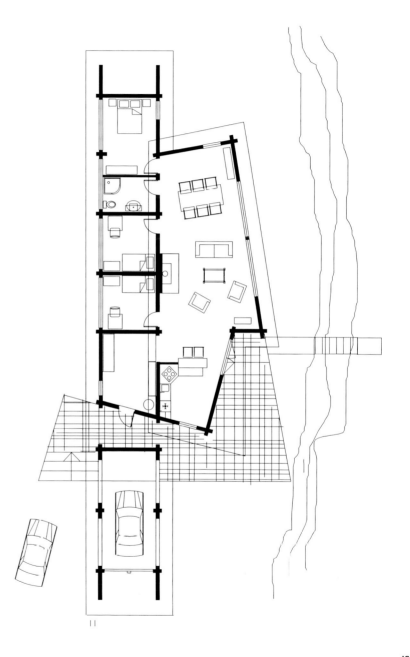

11

I

Villa von Bagh is located in Sotkamo, near Kajaani, on the banks of Lake Nuasjärvi. It was designed to accommodate a family of four during their vacations throughout the year—family holidays in the summer and short stays or working periods during winter.

The site for the house is remote and so early planning also had to take into account the area's freezing winter conditions. Temperatures can fall to as low as -40°F (-40°C)

in Sotkamo. For example, the building is divided into three volumes and resembles a tiny village or cluster of houses. This design maximizes on the interior's warmth and insulation, which can circulate between the building's tightly knit volumes

As the owners stay only occasionally during the winter months, the home's electrical heating was designed to maintain a minimum temperature of 50°F (10°C) when the house is empty. This system counters the harsh and corrosive elements of Sotkamo

2

3

winters' sub-zero temperatures. The heating system can also be controlled by a telephone impulse, which may be activated hours before the family comes to stay. When in use, the oven and wood-burning stove radiate warmth throughout the house as well.

To solve the issue of snow build-up on the roof of the house in winter, particularly when visits to the home are irregular, the roof's steep form has been designed to ensure that snow simply slides off. Similarly, unusually long eaves shelter entrance areas to the house so that

continued

1   Elevation facing Lake Nuasjärvi

2   Steeply sloped roof design
    prevents snow build-up

3   Exterior view toward living area

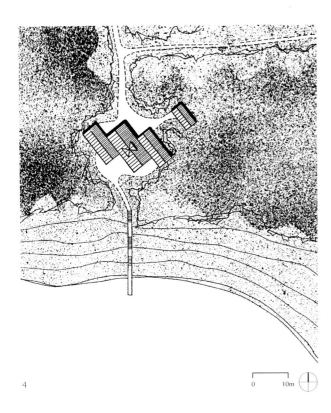

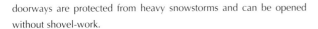

0   10m

4

doorways are protected from heavy snowstorms and can be opened without shovel-work.

The house is situated in beautiful scenery facing the lake and windows have been kept large, purposefully, to enjoy the views. The house's volumes were also juxtaposed to provide different views, while sheltered patios and seating areas were designed to make suitable and varied vantage points. To avoid loss of warmth in the winter, thermal glass was used for the home's large glazed areas.

5

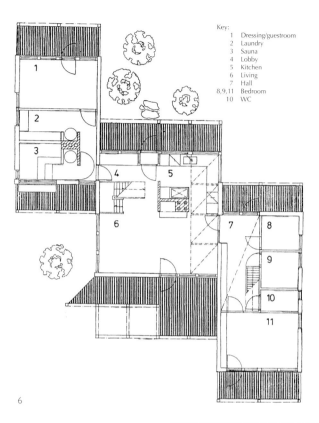

Key:
1   Dressing/guestroom
2   Laundry
3   Sauna
4   Lobby
5   Kitchen
6   Living
7   Hall
8,9,11   Bedroom
10   WC

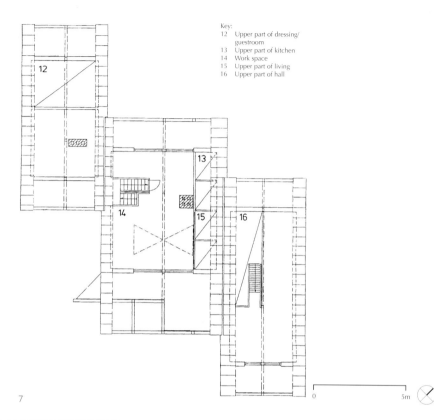

Key:
12   Upper part of dressing/
     guestroom
13   Upper part of kitchen
14   Work space
15   Upper part of living
16   Upper part of hall

6

7

0   5m

4   Site plan
5   Kitchen has an airy and
    transparent ambience
6   Ground floor plan
7   First floor plan
8&9   Living

Photography: Hannu Koivisto

8

9

In the Toronto garden suburb of Don Mills, 1960s ranch bungalows and their surrounding landscaping are being levelled and replaced by substantial, clumsy, historically referential, 'monster' houses. These houses form the new ideal suburban dream house. However, the L-shaped Weathering Steel House is in direct contrast to this context. Materially rich, dark, and abstract, it creates a clear threshold to the world within, to the site it creates, and to the ravine edge over which it looks.

A reflecting pool and swimming pool beyond are embedded into the house's center and form the intermediary between the building and its surrounding landscape. Toronto often experiences sub-zero temperatures in winter so pools are covered for six months of the year. Water is kept circulating year-round and only heated when the temperature drops below freezing. The benefits to the experience of the house are remarkable—as steam, ice, and the shift in temperature are registered against the winter water.

2

3

Toronto is situated on the northern shore of Lake Ontario—part of a large freshwater system known as the Great Lakes. The site's adjacency to this body of water creates a technically challenging climatic condition ranging from -40°F (-40°C) to 104°F (+40°C). The passive solar design of this project responds directly to this challenge by placing few windows and much of the service and circulation on the north side. Public rooms are located on the

continued

1 Ravine elevation in winter
2 Reflecting pool with house
   beyond in winter
3 North elevation in winter
   Photography: Michael Awad

4

5

6

4   Reflecting pool in winter
    Photography: Michael Awad
5   Exterior view looking toward reflecting pool
6   Interior view behind weathering steel wall
7   View of second-floor inverted bay window on
    north elevation
8   Stair to upper level
9   Living area with reflection of lily pads on wooden ceiling
10 View of reflecting pool looking toward ravine
    Photography: James Dow

south side to take advantage of solar gain and to benefit from views of the verdant ravine and city skyline beyond.

The design process began with meetings with the building envelope consultant Dr Ted Kesik (also the project's mechanical engineer) allowing the firm to carefully examine the interlocked relationship between life-cycle costing and capital cost. This project invests in the building envelope including double-glazed windows with a mylar layer in between,

which take advantage of the orientation on the north or south sides. In conjunction, insulation was added on walls and roof surfaces with consideration to the performance of the wall assembly. These decisions allow for reduced sizing and loads for the building's heating and cooling system.

The building cladding is weathering steel chosen for its direct interaction with nature, allowing the richly textured skin to darken slowly. The cladding is designed as a rain screen

7

9

8

10

system on an underlying 5.9-inch (150-millimeter) stud wall with 0.7 inch (18-millimeter) plywood sheathing and a waterproof membrane. In addition to bat insulation between studs, 1.5 inches (37 millimeters) of semi-rigid insulation was placed on the outer face of the waterproof membrane and an 0.7-inch (18-millimeter) continuous air space between the 2.2- by 4.9-inch (56- by 125-millimeter) vertical channels that carry the cladding panels and define the deeply recessed joints.

Because weathering steel is usually made in large sections for bridges and other civil engineering works, the channels and all the fixed components of this cladding system were break-formed from weathering steel plate.

191

The information and illustrations in this publication have been prepared and supplied by the entrants. While all reasonable efforts have been made to source the required information and ensure accuracy, the publishers do not, under any circumstances, accept responsibility for errors, omissions and representations expressed or implied.